2/10

DEMCO

DOMINICAN REPUBLIC

in Pictures

Christine Zuchora-Walske

Twenty-First Century Books

Contents

Website address: www.lernerbooks.com

Twenty-First Century Books
A division of Lerner Publishing Group, Inc.
241 First Avenue North
Minneapolis, MN 55401 U.S.A.

web enhanced @ www.vgsbooks.com

Library of Congress Cataloging-in-Publication Data

Zuchora-Walske, Christine.
    Dominican Republic in pictures / by Christine Zuchora-Walske.
        p.   cm. — (Visual geography series)
    Includes bibliographical references and index.
    ISBN 978-0-8225-8569-5 (lib. bdg. : alk. paper)
    1. Dominican Republic—Pictorial works—Juvenile literature. I. Title.
F1936.3.Z83 2008
    972.93—dc22   2007021325

Manufactured in the United States of America
1 2 3 4 5 6 - PA - 13 12 11 10 09 08

INTRODUCTION

Despite a long history of poverty and political strife, the Dominican Republic is a nation of stunning beauty and rich culture. It shares the Caribbean island of Hispaniola with Haiti. It also shares with Haiti and its other neighbors a common history of Native American, European, and African influences.

But despite this shared history, geography, and culture, the Dominican Republic's relations with its neighbors—and among its own people—have been stormy. From the day Christopher Columbus arrived in 1492 through most of the twentieth century, the nation has known few periods of peaceful government.

Spanish explorers first took over and then enslaved the population of Taino, a people who had thrived on Hispaniola for fifteen hundred years. Pirates often raided the colony. Spain and France fought over—and eventually divided—the island because of its location along trade routes between the Old and New Worlds. When slaves wrested control of Haiti from France, they took over the Dominican Republic too.

The country finally became independent in 1844. But that event triggered more than one hundred chaotic years of dictatorship, civil war, voluntary recolonization, military occupation, and political and financial power struggles.

The most memorable entry in this long list of troubles is the thirty-one–year tyranny of Rafael Leónidas Trujillo Molina. His regime, which began in 1930, made some economic and social improvements. However, these achievements came at a high cost. Trujillo ignored human rights, eliminated political opponents, and funneled most of the nation's new income to his own family.

Since Trujillo's assassination in 1961 and the following civil war, the Dominican Republic has made a fresh beginning. Ironically, the Dominican most consider responsible for this hopeful change—Joaquín Vidella Balaguer y Ricardo—was very close to Trujillo. Balaguer came to power via U.S. support and continued to lead a checkered political life. But Dominicans eventually elected him to the presidency a total of six times.

Dominican Republic

International border
Capital city
City

0   40 Miles
0   40 KM

N

TORTUGA ISLAND

GONÂVE ISLAND

HAITI

Artibonite River

Manzanillo Bay

Monte Cristi

Soile River

Lake Enriquillo

BEATA ISLAND

Yaque del Norte River

Puerto Plata

Santiago de los Caballeros

La Vega

Camú River

Yuna River

Yaque del Sur River

Neiba Bay

Ozama River

Bajos de Haina

Santo Domingo

Punta Caucedo

San Pedro de Macorís

Samaná Bay

La Romana

Higüey

SAONA ISLAND

Punta Cana

Mona Passage

MONA ISLAND

Puerto Rico (UNITED STATES)

ATLANTIC OCEAN

Caribbean Sea

Inset map

UNITED STATES

Gulf of Mexico

MEXICO

PACIFIC OCEAN

ATLANTIC OCEAN

CUBA

BAHAMAS

JAMAICA

HAITI

DOMINICAN REPUBLIC

Puerto Rico

Caribbean Sea

SOUTH AMERICA

0   500 Miles
0   500 KM

In the late 1960s and early 1970s, foreign aid and investment—as well as high prices for sugar, one of the country's main exports—helped the Dominican Republic rebuild its economy and restore order. From the late 1970s through the early 1990s, a drop in sugar prices hurt the economy. In the late 1990s, the economy boomed with growing tourism, telecommunications, and manufacturing. Massive bank fraud caused an economic crash in 2003, but by 2005 the nation was on the road to recovery.

The Dominican Republic still faces some serious challenges. These include a large foreign debt, constant electricity shortages, and a wide gulf between rich and poor. But its nine million citizens take strength from the giant strides their country has made during the past half century. The nation has free and fair elections, peaceful self-government, a diversified economy, and good international relations. It has put chaos and violence in the past and strives toward a peaceful, prosperous future.

 Visit www.vgsbooks.com for links to websites with additional information about the Dominican Republic.

THE LAND

The Dominican Republic shares the island of Hispaniola with Haiti. Hispaniola is part of the Greater Antilles. This is a group of islands that also includes Cuba and Jamaica to the west and Puerto Rico to the east. The Bahamas and the Atlantic Ocean lie to the north of Hispaniola. The Caribbean Sea lies to the south.

The Dominican Republic occupies the eastern two-thirds of Hispaniola. The nation covers about 18,815 square miles (48,730 square kilometers)—roughly twice the area of Vermont. Its land is richly varied, with rugged mountains, rolling hills, fertile valleys, coastal plains, and superb beaches. The territory includes several islands, of which Saona Island and Beata Island off the southern coast are the largest.

Topography

The backbone of the nation is the Cordillera Central. This is a mountain range that runs from northwest to southeast between the Haitian

border and the southern coast. The highest peak in this range, Pico Duarte, is 10,164 feet (3,098 meters) above sea level. It's named after Juan Pablo Duarte, a nineteenth-century independence leader. Rugged foothills lead up to the broad range.

West of Hispaniola, the Cordillera Central drops beneath the waters of the Windward Passage between Haiti and Cuba. It rises again to form the Sierra Maestra, a mountain range in eastern Cuba. East of Hispaniola, the Cordillera Central sinks beneath the Mona Passage. It reemerges as Puerto Rico's Cordillera Central.

Several smaller mountain ranges parallel the Dominican Republic's Cordillera Central. Near the northern coast lies the Cordillera Septentrional. The Sierra de Neiba and Sierra de Baoruco in the southwest are extensions of the Massif de la Selle, a range that stretches along southern Haiti. The Cordillera Oriental lies in the east.

The Cordillera Central blocks rain clouds blowing southward across the region. This makes the southwestern region quite arid.

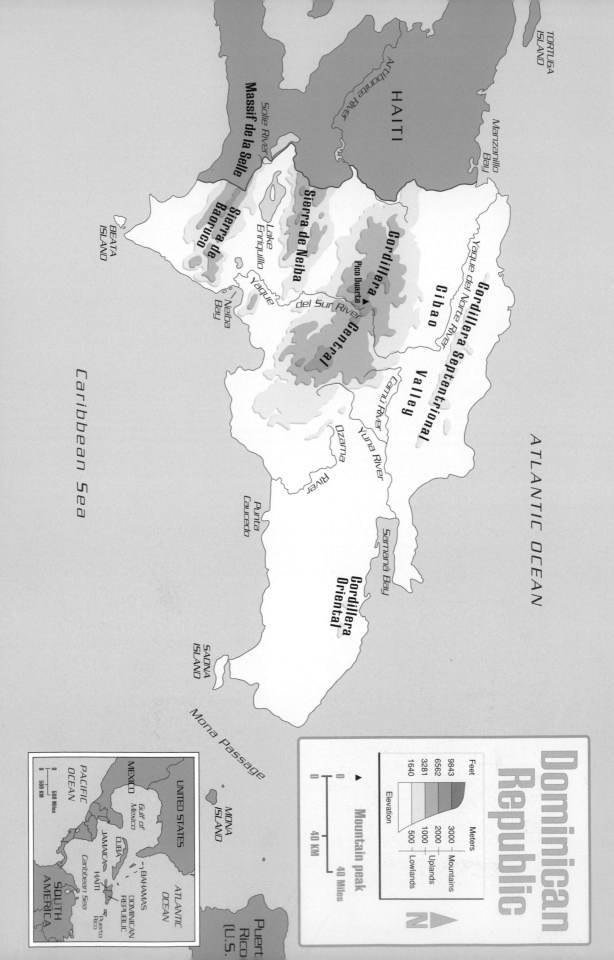

Within the Cordillera Central, residents of the many small valleys practice subsistence farming (growing just enough food to feed their families).

To the north, between the Cordillera Central and the Cordillera Septentrional, stretches the fertile Cibao Valley. This area is not only the breadbasket of the nation but also one of the most productive farming regions in the Caribbean. Its fields produce coffee, tobacco, cacao, corn, rice, beans, wheat, plantains (a type of banana), and many other grains, fruits, vegetables, and spices. Its pastures feed the nation's cattle. The valley's harvest is vitally important to the well-being both of the Dominican Republic and of its Caribbean neighbors.

Coastal plains dominate the eastern Dominican Republic north and south of the Cordillera Oriental. The heavily populated plains include sugarcane plantations, hundreds of miles of white-sand beaches, and the nation's capital city, Santo Domingo.

Rivers, Lakes, and Bays

The Dominican Republic has few large rivers. None of them is fully navigable. The longest river, the Yaque del Norte, begins on the northern slopes of the Cordillera Central. It flows northwestward through the Cibao Valley and empties into the Atlantic Ocean at Manzanillo Bay, near the Haitian border.

The **Yaque del Norte River** irrigates some rugged terrain in the Cordillera Central. To learn more about this beautiful island nation go to www.vgsbooks.com for links.

The country's two other main rivers are the Yuna-Camú system and the Yaque del Sur. The Yuna and Camú rivers, like the Yaque del Norte, rise on the northern slopes of the Cordillera Central. But they flow eastward, join, and empty into the Atlantic Ocean at Samaná Bay. The Yaque del Sur starts on the southern slopes. It flows southward and empties into the Caribbean Sea at Neiba Bay.

The Dominican Republic has many small rivers. Among these are the Ozama, the Artibonite, and the Solie. All three begin in the Cordillera Central. The Ozama River flows southward, emptying into the Caribbean Sea at Santo Domingo. The Artibonite is Hispaniola's longest river. Most of its length flows westward through Haiti, but it begins in the Dominican Republic. The Solie River became famous when it flooded in May 2004. This flood displaced and killed thousands of Dominicans and Haitians.

Lake Enriquillo lies in the southwest near the Haitian border. It's the largest inland body of water in the Caribbean. Its area varies from 77 to 102 square miles (200 to 265 square km) depending on rainfall and evaporation. The lake's surface is also the lowest point in the Caribbean. Its elevation varies too, but averages 131 feet (40 m) below sea level. The lake is very salty. It's one of the world's few saltwater lakes where crocodiles live.

Lake Enriquillo hosts one of the largest known populations of American crocodiles. This lake is the saltiest place American crocodiles live. It's about three times as salty as the sea.

Oceangoing vessels can load and unload cargo at several seaports, including Bajos de Haina, Santo Domingo, Punta Caucedo, San Pedro de Macorís, and La Romana on the southern coast. Monte Cristi and Puerto Plata are major seaports on the northern coast. The Dominican Republic's only large body of protected ocean water is Samaná Bay in the northeast.

Climate

The Dominican Republic has a tropical maritime climate. Its temperature varies more by location and time of day than by season. Its average annual temperature is 77°F (25°C). Highs of 104°F (40°C) are common in the valleys. Lows of 32°F (0°C) are common in the mountains.

The country's seasons are less a matter of temperature than of rainfall. The rainy season varies somewhat by location but generally runs from May through November. Rain often comes in short downpours followed by clear skies and cooler temperatures.

Because the wind usually blows from the north and east, mountain slopes facing in those directions get more rain than those facing south and west. The Cordillera Central tends to block windblown rain clouds, creating two distinct zones. The area north and east of the Cordillera Central is well watered and lush. The area south and west of the Cordillera Central gets far less rain and is very desertlike.

The island of Hispaniola lies within an area prone to tropical storms. These storms generally occur between June and November, bringing strong winds and heavy rain. Sometimes the storms develop into hurricanes. In September 1998, Hurricane Georges caused widespread destruction and death when it hit the Dominican Republic's heavily populated southern coast east of Santo Domingo.

Flora and Fauna

The Dominican Republic is home to a stunning array of plants and animals. This biodiversity is due to three main factors. Its island isolation has encouraged evolution of new species over millions of years. Its varied land and climate provide many different habitats. And during recent centuries, its location has made it a popular stop for travelers, who have introduced nonnative flora and fauna.

The Dominican Republic's natural biomes (major habitats) range from the very dry to the very wet. Thorn trees, cacti, and agave are plentiful in the arid southwest. Subtropical forest—including mahogany and royal palm trees—is the most common biome. This type of forest exists in many of the nation's valleys. Higher elevations have mountain forest vegetation, with both pines and palms. Small stands of tropical rain forest survive at the eastern end of the Cibao Valley. Mangrove swamps and coconut palms line coastal areas. Off the coast, shallow waters and abundant coral reefs create the perfect home for a great variety of sea life.

Many microhabitats exist among these major ones. The Dominican Republic also has vast tracts of cropland and pasture in addition to its natural vegetation. Flowering and fruiting plants—including orchids, royal poinciana, frangipani, mango, banana, papaya, passion fruit, and guava—grow nearly everywhere.

The Dominican Republic's fauna is as varied as its flora. Hundreds of bird species, including several dozen unique to Hispaniola, live there. Some of the country's colorful and interesting bird residents are the frigate bird, the Hispaniolan lizard-cuckoo, the roseate spoonbill, and many kinds of parrots. The island is also home to many different snakes, turtles, and other reptiles, from the tiny Jaragua lizard to the hefty rhinoceros iguana to the giant American crocodile.

A scuba diver studies the coral in **Laguna Pepe, a freshwater cave** near the eastern coast of the Dominican Republic. The cathedral-like cave is 160 feet (49 m) wide and 65 feet (20 m) high.

The population of wild land mammals has never been large, but it does include two endangered species that live nowhere else. These are the hutia (a tree rodent) and the solenodon (a venomous creature that looks like a huge shrew). The most common wild mammal is the mongoose. Europeans introduced this ferretlike animal to control the rats their ships had brought to Hispaniola. Unfortunately, the mongooses ignored the rats and gobbled up native birds, mammals, and reptiles instead. Modern Dominicans consider the mongoose a pest.

Dominican waters are famous for their marine mammals. These include dolphins, manatees, and humpback whales. The shallows abound with beautiful corals, sponges, shellfish, tropical fish, and sea turtles.

Natural Resources

The Dominican Republic has a variety of mineral resources. The country produces bauxite (aluminum ore), cement, nickel, gypsum (used in many building materials), limestone, marble, salt, sand and gravel, and steel. Among these industrial minerals, nickel is the most important. The nation also has deposits of gold, silver, zinc, and copper, which it has mined in varying degrees throughout its history. Of these precious minerals, gold has been the most important and is likely to remain so.

The Dominican Republic's energy resources are limited. Though it has some coal and oil reserves, it doesn't extract these fuels. Instead, it relies heavily on imported oil (oil bought from other countries) to generate power. Several of the country's rivers have hydroelectric dams, but these supply only a small fraction of the nation's energy.

The Dominican Republic's key natural resource is land. Its fertile soil and mild climate have made it a very productive agricultural nation. Also, many valuable trees—including mahogany, lignum vitae, satinwood, juniper, and pine—are native to Hispaniola. However, logging and farming have destroyed most of the Dominican Republic's native forest. (Experts estimate native forest loss of up to 90 percent.) This deforestation has caused widespread loss of soil fertility, erosion (wearing away) of topsoil, and coastal damage.

Environmental Issues

During the centuries after Europeans arrived on Hispaniola, its population slowly, steadily grew and settled the entire island. This ever-growing population needed food, shelter, and other means of survival. To supply their needs, people cut down almost all of Hispaniola's native trees. Residents did this both to clear farmland and for the wood's many valuable uses.

Deforestation severely damaged the country's environment. Heavy agriculture depleted the soil's nutrients, leading to more clearing as people searched for fertile land. Topsoil washed away by the ton, choking rivers and estuaries (where rivers empty into the sea) and burying coral reefs. Water quality and availability suffered. And as suitable habitat dwindled, so did wildlife.

In the late 1960s, deforestation reached a crisis point. Experts predicted that the Dominican Republic's remaining forest would vanish by the 1990s. Dominicans listened to this warning. In 1967 they outlawed commercial logging. In the 1980s, they dramatically slowed deforestation and began reforestation efforts. They set aside more than 10 percent of the nation's land in national parks and passed laws to protect the environment. By 2005 28 percent of the Dominican Republic had been forested.

Excess rain runoff due to deforestation was a key cause of the disastrous May 2004 flood in Hispaniola. This flood killed about nine hundred Dominicans and Haitians and left about fifteen thousand more homeless.

However, environmental problems persist. Much of the damage already done—especially topsoil loss and coastal ruin—is irreversible. And agricultural deforestation continues at a rate that nearly cancels out reforestation. Enforcing environmental laws is difficult, and widespread poverty leaves many Dominicans with no choice but to cut trees so they can grow food to survive.

The Dominican Republic faces new environmental challenges too. Since the 1950s, its population has steadily shifted into the cities. At the same time, the nation has been developing its tourism industry aggressively. As more and more people move to the cities, they increase the amount of pollution. And as more and more foreigners visit the Dominican Republic, they tread heavily on this beautiful— but fragile—country.

Fortunately, both Dominicans and concerned outsiders are aware of these problems and are trying to solve them. For example, the government is developing ways to put its environmental policy into practice. Public and private organizations are establishing programs that address both deforestation and rural poverty. And there's growing support for ecotourism, which helps the Dominican Republic earn income without destroying its natural resources.

In 2006 Bajos de Haina earned notoriety as one of the world's most polluted places. A battery recycling plant contaminated the city's soil. Research showed that more than 90 percent of local children had unsafe lead levels in their blood and that 33 percent of children had severe lead poisoning.

▶ Cities

SANTO DOMINGO is the nation's capital and its largest city. It's located on the Dominican Republic's southern coast at the mouth of the Ozama River. About 2.6 million people live in the city proper. The population of the entire metropolitan area is about 3.6 million. This city is the center of the nation's political, cultural, and economic life. Its economy is supported mainly by services and manufacturing.

Christopher Columbus's brother Bartholomew founded Santo Domingo in the late 1490s. It is the oldest continuously inhabited European settlement in the New World. Its history parallels the dramatic history of the Dominican Republic. Since the city's founding, it has witnessed the launch of Spanish conquest in the New World as well as piracy, occupation by various foreign powers, dictatorship, industrialization, the birth of Dominican democracy, and a modern period of rapid growth.

Santo Domingo's long and colorful history is evident in its structures. Its Colonial Zone is home to dozens of the oldest streets, buildings, and institutions in the New World. Outside this area lies the modern city, which includes high-rise apartment buildings, hotels, luxury housing, office buildings, shopping centers, and port facilities.

Santo Domingo's port includes an artificial harbor that is accessible to most commercial and passenger ships.

On the margins of the city are vast slums, where dwellings built of discarded materials house poor families.

SANTIAGO DE LOS CABALLEROS, the Dominican Republic's second-largest city, lies on the Yaque del Norte River in the heart of the Cibao Valley. Because of the city's location, many of its residents work in processing and shipping local farm products. About 830,000 people live in the city proper. The population of the entire metropolitan area is about 1.5 million.

Santiago's history is as long and colorful as Santo Domingo's. Like the capital, Santiago was founded in the late 1490s by Bartholomew Columbus. An earthquake destroyed it in 1562, the French looted it in 1689, the Haitians sacked it in 1803, and another earthquake damaged it in 1842. In 1844 it was the site of an important battle in the Dominican Republic's war for independence from Haiti. In 1863 Dominican rebels burned the city to the ground to drive out attacking Spanish forces.

Unlike Santo Domingo, Santiago retains little of its colonial architecture. But like the capital, it is growing very rapidly.

Visit www.vgsbooks.com for links to websites with additional information about the Dominican Republic. Learn about efforts to preserve Dominican natural resources and get information about traveling around the country.

HISTORY AND GOVERNMENT

Around 5000 B.C., natives of Central and South America began migrating to the Caribbean islands, including Hispaniola. By A.D. 1000, Hispaniola had a well-developed Taino culture. Other native groups were present in the area too. But for the next five centuries, the Taino flourished on Hispaniola. They called the island Quisqueya.

The Quisqueyan Taino were a prosperous, well-organized, and peaceful people. They farmed the island's fertile soil, hunted in its forests, and fished its teeming waters. They lived in villages made up of *bohíos*, large thatched dwellings that housed extended families. Five caciques (chiefs) ruled the different regions of Quisqueya. At the end of the 1400s, these five Taino groups were on the verge of unifying. Their only enemies were the warlike Caribs, who often attacked from neighboring islands.

◉ The Taino-Spanish Encounter

In 1492 the Taino encountered a new threat: the Spanish. Christopher Columbus and his crew arrived at Quisqueya in December of that year.

The Taino greeted them with generosity. By and large, the Spanish returned this greeting with ignorance, violence, and greed.

Like most Europeans of the time, Spanish explorers viewed non-Europeans as inferiors. They saw the Taino culture as primitive and pagan (heathen and sinful). They believed they had a duty to civilize the Taino and convert them to Catholicism. They also believed they had a right to claim Quisqueya (which they renamed Hispaniola), as well as its people and abundant resources, for the Spanish Empire.

The Spaniards often dealt brutally with their island hosts. Treachery, kidnapping, rape, torture, enslavement, and murder were common. Some Taino not killed outright by Spaniards chose suicide. Many others died of starvation, exhaustion, and disease.

By the early 1500s, only a fraction of Hispaniola's Taino population remained. The survivors either fled or blended into Spanish colonial society as best they could. Their culture and their bloodline went underground—alive, but unrecognized—for the next five hundred years.

The Early Colony

When Columbus returned to Spain after his first visit to Hispaniola in 1492, he left thirty-nine men behind at a fort called La Navidad on the northern coast. He returned in December 1493 to find all the men dead. They had raided the Tainos and kidnapped many women. The Taino had responded by killing the Spaniards and burning their fort to the ground.

In 1494 Columbus established a second settlement, La Isabela, to the east of La Navidad. But internal fighting and the flight of Taino laborers doomed this settlement. Two years later, the Spanish population had splintered and abandoned La Isabela for other regions.

One group of settlers followed Columbus's brother, Bartholomew, to a natural seaport on the southern coast. They named this new town—and the colony as a whole—Santo Domingo. It didn't immediately prosper, but it did endure, going on to become the oldest continuously inhabited European settlement in the New World.

As they had done at La Isabela, the Spaniards continued to seize Taino land and enslave the Taino people. Christopher Columbus explored more of the Caribbean, continuing his brilliant career as a navigator. But he failed miserably as governor of Santo Domingo. In 1500 the colonists sent Columbus home to Spain in chains and disgrace. (The king and queen later released him from prison.) From 1501 to 1509, Nicolás de Ovando ruled Santo Domingo with an iron hand and made it into a profitable colony.

Colonial Development

Hundreds of Spanish immigrants followed Ovando to the lush island to establish farms, ranches, and gold mines. Sugar production flourished. So did crops of European fruits, vegetables, and grains. Imported chickens, pigs, sheep, goats, cattle, donkeys, and horses quickly multiplied.

In 1509 the king of Spain appointed Diego Columbus, Christopher's son, as governor of Santo Domingo. Diego ruled the island until his death in 1526. During his first two years as governor, the Spanish crown became concerned that he was acting mainly in self-interest. The monarchy limited his authority in 1511 by establishing an *audiencia*, a group of judges representing the crown.

In 1516 a group of friars (Catholic brothers)—among the few who were shocked by the colonists' abuse of the Taino—convinced the crown to allow reforms. The friars had just begun to free and resettle the Taino in self-governing villages when a smallpox epidemic broke out. The epidemic killed thousands of Taino and effectively destroyed their society. The friars gave up their plan.

Diego Columbus, Christopher Columbus's son, ruled Spain's holdings in the Americas from 1509 to 1526. He may have made important decisions in this tiled courtyard at El Alcázar de Colón, Diego's home in Santo Domingo.

Officially the Columbus family (represented by Diego's son Luis) kept authority over Santo Domingo until 1536, when it sold its rights back to the crown. In practice, however, the audiencia grew into the most powerful arm of colonial government. By 1524 the Royal Audiencia of Santo Domingo had authority over all of Spain's colonies in the Caribbean, Mexico, Central America, and the northern coast of South America.

In the early 1500s, Santo Domingo served as the key base from which Spain extended its empire in the New World. But in the mid-1500s, Santo Domingo began to decline, mainly because its gold mines were exhausted. Meanwhile, Spain's new colonies, Mexico and Peru, proved to be bountiful sources of gold and silver. This wealth captured the attention of both the crown and Spanish settlers.

As Spain's focus turned to Mexico and Peru, Santo Domingo's focus turned to sugarcane and cattle. The rise of sugarcane plantations led to the import of African slaves. Soon the African population far outnumbered the Spanish and Taino populations. Many slaves escaped and formed communities in the mountains. The Spanish called these fugitives *cimarrones*.

▶ Isolation

From the mid-1500s through the 1600s, the colony of Santo Domingo struggled. As Spain's priorities shifted westward, its main trading route shifted northward. Havana, Cuba, replaced Santo Domingo as

In the sixteenth and seventeenth centuries, Spain controlled the Americas. The Spanish were mining staggering amounts of gold and silver there—especially in Mexico and Peru. The huge Spanish treasure shipments from the New World to the Old World attracted pirates all along the route from the Caribbean to Seville, Spain. Tortuga Island, at Hispaniola's northeastern end, served as a headquarters of Caribbean piracy during this period.

Spain's primary Caribbean seaport. At the same time, the Caribbean Sea was a haven for pirates. Spanish ships began traveling in fleets for safety. Few were willing to risk a dangerous solo trip to Santo Domingo, which was off the main route. To make matters worse, Spain forbade Santo Domingo to trade with other countries. As a result, the colony became isolated. Its economy suffered as markets for Santo Domingo's raw goods dwindled.

The colonists were in dire need of manufactured goods from Europe, as well as markets for selling their raw goods. So while the city of Santo Domingo languished in the south, illegal trade with foreigners flourished in the north and west. In 1605, to calm angry Spanish merchants, Spain forcibly relocated the residents of northern and western Hispaniola to new settlements near the city. This act became known as the *devastaciones* (devastations). It financially ruined the relocated families, impoverished the entire colony, and left much of Hispaniola vulnerable to pirates, foreign settlers, and rebellious cimarrones.

Eventually, Spain simply abandoned western Hispaniola. In 1697, under the Treaty of Ryswick, Spain formally granted the western third of the island to France. Renamed Saint-Domingue, this area developed into one of the wealthiest of all New World colonies.

French and Haitian Occupation

During the 1700s, Spain's remaining colony of Santo Domingo gradually revived. Though it had lost one-third of its land to France and constantly fought further French encroachment, it also made money off the new French colony. As Saint-Domingue's population exploded and its economy boomed, it provided an ever-growing market for raw goods from its Spanish neighbor.

Santo Domingo's luck was improving, but Spain's was crumbling. As Spain lost power in Europe, it signed the Treaty of Basel with France in 1795. This treaty yielded the rest of Hispaniola to France for the return of captured Spanish territory in Europe.

Meanwhile, the colony of Saint-Domingue was in turmoil. Stirred by the principles of the French Revolution—liberty, brotherhood, and equality—slaves revolted and mulattoes (people of mixed European and African ancestry) pressed for an end to discrimination. Throughout the 1790s, whites, slaves, and mulattoes in Saint-Domingue battled for control of the colony. In 1800 freed slave and brilliant military leader François-Dominique Toussaint-Louverture gained the upper hand. Though Saint-Domingue was still officially a French colony, France had no control over Toussaint-Louverture.

France had not yet taken over Santo Domingo because of the chaos in Saint-Domingue. Toussaint-Louverture moved troops into Santo Domingo in 1800 and fully occupied it in 1801. He immediately freed its slaves and took steps to integrate the Spanish people and economy with the French one. By this time, thousands of Spaniards had fled to other Caribbean islands and to South America.

In 1802 French ruler Napoleon Bonaparte sent a large military force to Hispaniola. He wanted to wrest control of it from Toussaint-Louverture and reintroduce slavery. The French easily took over Santo Domingo, since the Spanish preferred domination by their long-time enemies to being ruled by blacks. Saint-Domingue, however, resisted fiercely. With help from various diseases, which claimed more than fifty thousand of Napoleon's soldiers, Toussaint-Louverture's troops defeated the French in late 1803. On January 1, 1804, Haiti declared its independence.

Unlike most people born into slavery, François-Dominique **Toussaint-Louverture** learned to read and write as a boy. Positions of responsibility on his owner's plantation gave him leadership experience. He used it to become a leader of the slave uprising on Haiti. He died in 1803.

The French retreated from Haiti but stayed in Santo Domingo. The weak French government had to defend itself constantly against Haitian invasions.

With British support, rebellious Spanish colonists in Santo Domingo threw out the French in 1809. Once again Santo Domingo became a Spanish colony.

Government incompetence marked the next twelve years of Santo Domingo's history. In 1821 local leaders, having had enough of Spanish rulers, seceded (withdrew) from Spain. They sought support for independence by offering to join Gran Colombia (which then included Colombia, Panama, Venezuela, and Ecuador). But Gran Colombia refused the offer.

Into the political vacuum stepped Jean-Pierre Boyer, president of Haiti. Boyer and the Haitian army occupied Santo Domingo in 1822, just after the colonists evicted the Spaniards.

Boyer ruled Haiti and Santo Domingo for the next twenty-one years. Despite his attempts to stimulate the economy, both former colonies grew poorer. The population of Santo Domingo dropped to about half the size it had been in 1800. The university in the city of Santo Domingo closed. Unused public schools and churches fell into disrepair.

▶ Independence, Annexation, and Power Struggles

When Boyer's rivals overthrew him in 1843, Juan Pablo Duarte led Santo Domingo in a rebellion against Haiti. By using guerrilla warfare (constantly shifting attacks, sabotage, and terrorism) and *caudillos* (military strongmen), Santo Domingo defeated Haiti's superior military. The most powerful caudillo was Pedro Santana Familias. Santana not only turned back the Haitians but also sent the idealistic Duarte into exile (forced him to leave the country).

In 1844 Santo Domingo declared its independence and renamed itself the Dominican Republic. Santana presided over widespread disorder until his opponents forced him to resign in 1848. The following year, Santana led the army to repel another threat from Haiti. He regained control of the government. But instead of taking on the presidency, Santana placed his fellow caudillo Buenaventura Báez in the office. Santana remained commander in chief of the armed forces.

For a time, both leaders sought outside support from Spain, France, Britain, and the United States. But none of those countries was interested in getting involved. In 1853 Báez quarreled with and outlawed Santana. Before the year was finished, Santana had retaken the presidency. Two years later, he repelled another invasion from Haiti. The next year, Báez deposed Santana. A year later, Santana retaliated by unseating Báez.

Buenaventura Báez served as the president of the Dominican Republic five times between 1849 and 1878. One of his goals was to convince France, the United States, or Spain to annex his country. None of these nations showed a long-lasting interest in doing so.

Spain saw in this power struggle an opportunity to regain some of its lost colonial influence. In 1861 it agreed to Santana's request for annexation (becoming a Spanish territory). Spain appointed Santana as captain general (military governor). However, few Dominicans shared Santana's desire for Spanish protection, and Santana found that it had greatly reduced his power. He resigned in 1862, leaving his Spanish successor to handle the already widespread rebellion.

Spanish forces on Hispaniola battled not only relentless guerilla warfare, but also rampant disease. The Spanish government at home was failing. It also faced U.S. displeasure at its renewed imperial ambitions. Unwilling and unable to challenge the United States—a nation powerfully armed after its Civil War (1861–1865)—and earning little money from the Dominicans, Spain withdrew in 1865.

Báez dominated the thirteen years after Spanish withdrawal. During this time, he nearly persuaded the United States to buy the Dominican Republic's Samaná Bay and Samaná Peninsula for a naval base. He also sought U.S. annexation. President Ulysses S. Grant supported this proposal, but the U.S. Senate rejected it.

The failure of annexation led to U.S. naval withdrawal from the area. As a result, Báez was overthrown. He managed a return to power in late 1876 for fourteen more months.

The Heureaux Years

After another brief period of turmoil, Báez's regime gave way to that of Ulises Heureaux. Heureaux was a military dictator who controlled the nation's affairs for almost two decades—sometimes as president and sometimes as minister of war. Heureaux's government, like earlier caudillo governments, mainly served its leader's interests and treated its opponents brutally. However, it did provide enough internal order to stimulate the economy.

The Heureaux years saw the completion of a few short railways, telegraph and cable lines, and better port facilities. But these modest improvements, combined with a drop in sugar prices and the expense of buying political loyalty, severely strained the country's financial resources. Its foreign debt increased tenfold.

Ulises Heureaux dressed lavishly for this official portrait. Much of the money his government borrowed from foreign countries went to support his personal extravagances and the administrative expenses of running a police state.

In 1888 Heureaux's government secured a large loan from Westendorp, a Dutch banking firm. To guarantee the loan, Westendorp officials managed Dominican customs (taxes that formed the country's main source of income), keeping 30 percent of revenues and delivering the rest to the Dominican government. In 1890 the firm provided another, even larger, loan.

In 1893, on the verge of bankruptcy, Westendorp sold its rights in the Dominican Republic to the U.S.-based San Domingo Improvement Company (SDIC). As a condition for this transfer, Heureaux demanded more large loans from SDIC. The foreign debt skyrocketed.

While Dominicans labored under Heureaux's tyranny, his government faced bankruptcy. SDIC managed the nation's finances poorly, which aggravated its money problems instead of relieving them. Fed up with oppression and financial chaos, rebels assassinated Heureaux in 1899.

◉ U.S. Involvement

For the next six years, the Dominican Republic suffered constant power struggles and ever-growing foreign debt. Each weak, short-lived government during this period borrowed money from abroad but repaid none of the money it owed. In 1901 the Dominican Republic kicked out SDIC for mismanagement.

The U.S. government came to SDIC's defense. The United States pointed to Dominican political and financial chaos as evidence of gross misconduct.

Meanwhile, European governments threatened military invasion to force payment of their citizens. These threats violated the Monroe Doctrine. The Monroe Doctrine states that the United States views any European attempt to control a Western Hemisphere nation as a hostile act against the United States

In 1904 U.S. president Theodore Roosevelt announced an amendment to the Monroe Doctrine that became known as the Roosevelt Corollary. This amendment alerted the world that if a Latin American state engaged in flagrant wrongdoing, the United States had the right to intervene in its internal affairs.

The Monroe Doctrine and the Roosevelt Corollary gave the U.S. government two reasons for stepping into Dominican affairs. In 1905 the Dominican Republic agreed to a U.S. takeover of Dominican finances. After delivering 45 percent of customs revenues to the Dominican government, the United States divided the remaining funds among the country's creditors. The agreement also authorized the United States to intervene in any situation that threatened the new financial arrangement.

Ramón Cáceres, one of Heureaux's assassins, headed the Dominican government from 1905 to 1911. This was a relatively stable period. Thanks to sound financial management and vigorous agricultural development, the nation's debt shrank dramatically and its income grew. The government set in motion a much-needed program of public works.

But not all Dominicans were happy with Cáceres's government. Some landowners and businesspeople believed his economic policies favored foreign companies. Others resented his post-Heureaux political housecleaning. In 1911 a group of rebels assassinated Cáceres. This event threw the country back into confusion.

To bring matters under control, the United States forced president Eladio Victoria out of office in 1912 by withholding the Dominican share of customs revenues. In 1914 the United States pressured the Dominicans into holding a presidential election. Juan Isidro Jiménez, an aging politician, won. A revolt erupted immediately, and Jiménez resigned.

Rule by the U.S. Marines

In 1916 the United States, led by President Woodrow Wilson, began to take control of the Dominican Republic—just as the year before it had taken over Haiti. After the U.S. Marines landed, the Dominican

U.S. Marines land at Santo Domingo in 1916.

congress elected a presumably docile provisional president, Francisco Henríquez y Carvajal. Henríquez surprised the United States by refusing to act as its puppet. He tried to salvage Dominican rights in the face of a powerful foreign military presence.

On November 29, 1916, U.S. naval officer Harry S. Knapp assumed complete authority over the Dominican government on the grounds that the country needed help maintaining law and order. The United States—on the brink of entering World War I (1914–1918)—also claimed that the Dominican Republic was vulnerable to German invasion.

For the next six years, the Dominican government was a military dictatorship run by U.S. officers who were poorly qualified for their jobs. They sent home the Dominican congress and dismissed many

U.S. Marines patrol Santo Domingo from the Ozama River in 1919. To learn more about the history and government of the Dominican Republic, visit www.vgsbooks.com for links.

judges. The soldiers dealt harshly with guerrilla resistance and organized a large, well-trained local force called the National Police.

The period of United States occupation brought some material benefits. High prices for Dominican sugar and cacao (beans from which chocolate is made) provided money to pay foreign debts and run the government. This money also helped the government meet its goal of building schools and other much-needed public works, such as sewers and roads. Mosquito-elimination campaigns and other sanitation measures improved public health.

Dominicans applauded the progress but chafed under foreign rule. Some accused the United States of juggling landownership laws to help Americans take over desirable plantations. Dominicans also accused U.S. military personnel of brutality and racism. The United States censored the Dominican press during World War I and tightened censorship after the war.

By the end of 1920, the occupation had inflamed Dominican patriotism to the point of rebellion. Near the end of his second term in office, Wilson announced that the U.S. Marines would withdraw.

For the next four years, Wilson's successor, Warren G. Harding, worked to safely restore Dominican self-rule. Matters to be settled included a way to continue payments on the Dominican Republic's foreign debt, a means to maintain control over the economy, and funds to support the National Police.

The resolution of these issues paved the way for popular elections. Horacio Vásquez, a veteran politician, assumed a four-year presidential term in July 1924. Two months later, the U.S. Marines departed.

The Trujillo Dictatorship

Dominicans enjoyed a stable government under Vásquez. A free Dominican press flourished, and the National Police maintained peace. Economic progress made the island attractive to foreign investors. A middle class emerged as the number of educated people grew.

But in 1926, a dispute erupted over whether the Dominican congress could legally extend Vásquez's term to 1930 and whether he could run for reelection then. The lack of an organized opposition party meant Vásquez easily won a longer term and the right to run for reelection. However, the president had not taken into account the National Police. This force had evolved into a powerful National Army under the leader he'd appointed: Rafael Trujillo.

In February 1930, when an uprising against Vásquez occurred in the Cibao Valley, Vásquez directed the army to deal with it. But Trujillo, conspiring secretly with the rebels, did nothing. A small rebel force marched into the capital, threw out Vásquez, and took over the government.

After the government rebuilt hurricane-ravaged Santo Domingo, **Rafael Trujillo** renamed the capital city Ciudad Trujillo (Trujillo City). Its name reverted to Santo Domingo after his assassination in 1961.

Trujillo recognized the rebel leader, Rafael Estrella Ureña, as provisional president. At the same time, Trujillo announced his candidacy for the May 1930 presidential election.

The election was neither peaceful nor free. Trujillo intimidated all opponents by persecuting, jailing, or assassinating them. This was an easy task, because the United States had disarmed the Dominican people during its occupation while generously arming the National Police.

Trujillo's bullying worked. On election day, he announced that he had triumphed. He rounded up his remaining opponents and killed them. Then Trujillo and his U.S.-trained army—which was loyal to him rather than to the principles of democracy—began an extremely brutal and corrupt thirty-one–year dictatorship.

From 1930 to 1961, Trujillo held the presidency most of the time and controlled the nation all the time. To glorify himself and silence his critics, he tightly reined the press and built a huge propaganda machine. To maintain his authority, he handed out both material and social rewards. He bought the loyalty of his handpicked officers and shrewdly secured the emotional attachment of the enlisted men. He also organized a personal police force that rivaled the National Police. Using this force, Trujillo found and killed his opponents both at home and abroad.

TRUJILLO'S HAITIAN GENOCIDE

The Dominican Republic's long struggle with Haiti left the exact location of its western border in question well into the early twentieth century. In 1929 the two nations finally signed a treaty fixing the border.

But tens of thousands of poor Haitians remained on the Dominican side. They worked on small farms, as laborers in the sugar industry, as domestic servants, or as small businessowners. These people functioned as an extension of Haiti—speaking its language, using its currency, and staying on the margins of the Dominican society and economy.

Trujillo found this situation intolerable. In October 1937, he ordered his army to kill all Haitians on sight. Up to eighteen thousand Haitians died in this act of genocide.

Although many people witnessed and protested the slaughter and although news of it traveled quickly around the globe, Trujillo never admitted to it. Instead he paid Haiti a few hundred thousand dollars for damages and injuries caused by the "frontier conflict" and resettled the border area with Dominicans.

The country seemed to prosper under Trujillo's leadership. His government paid off the foreign debt, built schools, paved roads, and modernized seaports. He reorganized industry and agriculture so the Dominican Republic could supply its own needs and stop relying on imports. But he took over most of the nation's profitable businesses. So the new wealth flowed directly into his personal treasury, not the nation's. While Trujillo and his family and friends grew rich, most Dominicans lived in fear and poverty.

After World War II (1939–1945), Trujillo's grip on the Dominican Republic began to slip. The United States no longer needed his cooperation to help defend Latin America from Nazi Germany, so it stopped ignoring his abuses. Evidence of the personal fortunes amassed by the Trujillo circle shocked the world. Accounts of Trujillo's brutality and repression angered both Dominicans and foreigners.

Trujillo supported an attempt to assassinate Venezuela's president Rómulo Betancourt in 1960. In response, the Organization of American States (OAS) voted to condemn Trujillo's regime and impose economic sanctions (trade restrictions). The international community was fed up with his family's obvious political and personal excesses. Early in 1961, the Dominican Republic's Catholic clergy even dared to denounce him. On the night of May 30, 1961, conspirators within Trujillo's government killed him in a highway ambush.

In the 1940s, Trujillo built the **National Palace in Santo Domingo.** Its dome is 112 feet (34 m) high and 59 feet (18 m) in diameter.

After Trujillo

After Trujillo's death, the United States quickly intervened. It stationed several warships just offshore to prevent the Trujillo family from regaining power and to discourage invasion by Cuba's new Communist leader, Fidel Castro. (A Communist is someone who supports a political system in which people own all property collectively.) The United States also gave advice and financial aid to help the Dominican government recover Trujillo family assets.

Joaquín Balaguer, a longtime associate of Trujillo, served as head of the first transitional council of state. A second council removed Balaguer, and he left the country. In a free, fair, and well-attended 1962 presidential election, the Dominican people chose a long-exiled liberal intellectual, Juan Bosch. Conservative clergy, military officers, landowners, and the U.S. government—all of them paranoid about the spread of Communism—were dismayed. In late 1963, before Bosch had served a year in office, a military coup (overthrow) replaced him with a group of three business leaders called the Triumvirate.

The new government lasted a year and a half thanks to U.S. support, but it was very unpopular. Many lower- and middle-class Dominicans feared a return to Trujillo-like oppression, and they backed a movement to restore Bosch's honestly elected liberal government.

On April 25, 1965, friends gather around **Juan Bosch** *(front right)*, the exiled president of the Dominican Republic, in his apartment in San Juan, Puerto Rico. They are listening to radio reports about a coup in the Dominican Republic that could restore Bosch to power.

On April 25, 1965, civil war erupted in Santo Domingo. Within three days the liberals had gained the upper hand. On April 28, 1965, U.S. president Lyndon Johnson ordered the marines to land in Santo Domingo. Johnson's public reason for this act was protecting U.S. citizens there. The underlying reason, however, was to prevent the Dominican Republic from becoming a Communist nation like Cuba. Several days later, the OAS voted to establish an Inter-American Peace Force of troops from the United States, Brazil, Honduras, Paraguay, and Costa Rica.

The bloodshed continued, however, and much of Santo Domingo was ruined. The war killed about four thousand people before its end in late August 1965. On September 3, Héctor García-Godoy took office as provisional president with a mandate to organize internationally supervised general elections in June 1966. While he did this, Balaguer and Bosch returned from exile to campaign for the presidency. Balaguer won a strong victory. In September 1966, foreign troops withdrew.

Soldiers from Honduras, part of the OAS force, arrive for **peacekeeping duty** in the Dominican Republic.

▶ The Balaguer Regime

Dominicans reelected Balaguer in 1970 and 1974. During his first twelve years as president, Balaguer's conservative government resembled those of Trujillo and earlier caudillos. Power and privilege relied on connection with the president. And because Balaguer was eager to maintain his position, his government silenced political opposition with military force.

Unlike Trujillo, Balaguer cultivated a good image abroad. And through skillful public relations at home, he took full credit for an upturn in the economy. Balaguer governed during a period of unusual prosperity fueled largely by U.S. aid. High prices for Dominican sugar, increased foreign investment, and rapid tourism growth were also helpful.

In the 1978 election, Balaguer ran against liberal Antonio Guzmán. When vote counting began to show that Guzmán would win, the Dominican army tried to stop the count. Balaguer ordered it to resume and calmly witnessed Guzmán's triumph. This election marked the first peaceful transfer of political power from one civilian party to another in twentieth-century Dominican history. In 1982 another liberal candidate, Salvador Jorge Blanco, won the presidential election.

Neither of these leaders could maintain the prosperity Dominicans had enjoyed in the late 1960s and early 1970s. A worldwide recession caused unemployment and a decline in foreign investment. Lower sugar prices—combined with a U.S. decision to reduce its import quotas for Dominican sugar—devastated the Dominican economy.

Voters returned Balaguer to power in 1986. And though he was going blind and his health was failing, Balaguer won again in 1990 and 1994.

But Balaguer's opponents called for an investigation of the 1994 election. The inquiry found that thousands of Dominicans—mostly liberals—were missing from the voter registry. A violent period of protests, strikes, and political turmoil followed. It ended with the Pact for Democracy, which the nation's political parties signed in August 1994. This agreement shortened Balaguer's term from four years to two years. It also prohibited future presidents from serving two terms in a row.

◉ Into a New Millennium

Leonel Fernández Reyna, a native Dominican who grew up in the United States and returned home to earn a law degree, won the Dominican presidency in 1996. After taking office, Fernández moved to improve Dominican-Haitian relations, which had been poor since the early 1800s. He pursued economic and judicial reform and

Dominican president Leonel Fernández Reyna addresses the United Nations General Assembly on September 20, 2006.

enhanced Dominican participation in international forums. He also focused on improving the nation's communication and information technology. From 1996 to 2000, the Dominican economy's growth rate was the highest in Latin America.

According to the Pact for Democracy, Fernández could not run for reelection in 2000. And since Fernández's policies hadn't improved most Dominicans' lives, voters rejected his right-hand man, Danilo Medina. They elected Hipólito Mejía instead.

Dominicans liked Mejía's folksy personality, but he presided over a dark time. The economy shrank dramatically after September 11, 2001. On this date, terrorist attacks on the United States struck a serious blow to the economy of the United States, the Dominican Republic's main trading partner. To make matters worse, in 2003 the country's three biggest private banks collapsed. Mejía's government bailed out the banks' depositors, a move that caused a massive fiscal shortfall. This shortfall led to inflation, currency devaluation, and higher taxes.

With a pledge to revive the Dominican economy, Fernández won the presidency again in 2004. And since the constitution was amended during Mejía's term to let a sitting president run for reelection, Fernández is eligible for another term. In 2007 he became an official candidate for the 2008 presidential election.

Government

The Dominican Republic is a representative democracy with three branches of government. The president, elected by popular vote for a four-year term, heads the executive branch. The legislative branch consists of a thirty-two–member Senate and a 150-member Chamber of Deputies. Both senators and deputies are elected by popular vote and serve four-year terms. A Supreme Court of appointed justices heads the judicial branch, which also includes courts of appeal, courts of first instance, and a judge for each municipality.

Administratively, the country is divided into thirty-one provinces and one district, whose governors are appointed by the president. The national district includes the capital city of Santo Domingo. The provinces, in turn, are divided into 154 municipalities.

Visit www.vgsbooks.com for links to websites with additional information about the history of the Dominican Republic. Read about government leaders and follow the country's continuing efforts toward peaceful relations with Haiti.

THE PEOPLE

The Dominican Republic is home to about nine million people. Researchers expect the population to exceed fourteen million by 2050— an increase of 57 percent. The population is growing about 1.7 percent per year.

The Dominican government generally views its rate of population growth as too high. So despite cultural resistance and opposition from the Catholic Church, the state supports family planning programs. These programs supply about 36 percent of modern contraceptives (birth control) used in the Dominican Republic.

An average of 479 people live in each square mile of the Dominican Republic. Dominicans are unevenly distributed between urban and rural areas. About 64 percent live in urban areas. Approximately one-half of this urban population (about one-third of the total population) lives in the National District (the area surrounding the capital city, Santo Domingo). The rest of the urban population lives in the cities and towns of the fertile lowlands. The Cibao Valley,

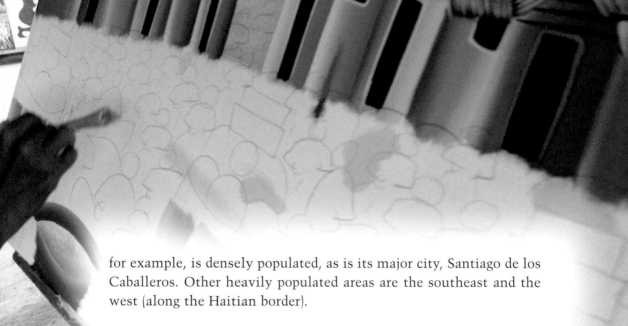

for example, is densely populated, as is its major city, Santiago de los Caballeros. Other heavily populated areas are the southeast and the west (along the Haitian border).

◉ Ethnic Groups

The people of the Dominican Republic are a rich ethnic mixture of European, African, and Taino bloodlines. Roughly 10 percent of Dominicans claim descent from only European—mainly Spanish—ancestors. About 15 percent claim only African descent. The remaining 75 percent are of mixed racial backgrounds. The nation's Taino heritage rests entirely within its mixed-race population.

Although the vast majority of Dominicans are multiracial, the nation has a long history of identifying itself as Spanish. This attitude is a natural result of Hispaniola's domination by Europeans during the past five centuries.

TAINO SURVIVAL

Nearly every history of the Dominican Republic written through the 1900s declared the Taino extinct. In the 1980s, scholars began to question this idea. They found evidence of Taino survival in Dominican historical documents and language. The nation's cooking, folk medicine, craft methods, spirituality, family life, festivals, popular culture, and genetic bloodlines also helped.

Spanish colonists had indeed killed thousands of Taino. But the Taino didn't disappear. The Spaniards wanted Hispaniola for themselves. Their seizure was easier to justify if they claimed the Taino were gone. Lack of native workers also provided an excuse to import African slaves. Once the Spanish had complete control, survival depended on blending into Spanish society.

A small number of Taino had survived, and their culture and genes had mixed with those of Spaniards and Africans. But because Taino heritage brought no benefit, it went unspoken. Eventually, Dominican society forgot its native origins.

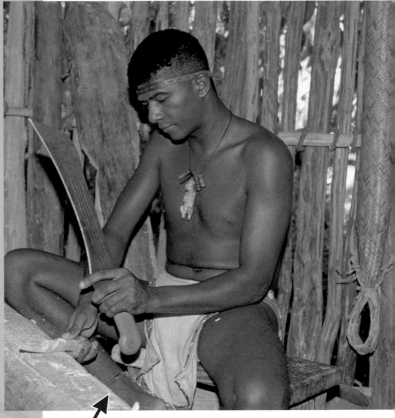

A young Dominican, dressed like his Taino ancestors, demonstrates a traditional craft.

Once the Spaniards wrested the island from its native population and began importing African slaves, it was far better to be Spanish than to be Taino or African. This reality led to a preference for light skin, straight hair, and "white" racial features.

Because of this preference, Dominicans tend to deny their non-European heritage and to look down on Native American and African racial feaures. Modern Dominicans with darker skin—especially those of Haitian descent—often suffer discrimination.

Socioeconomics

The Dominican Republic's ethnic divisions are subtle and complex, but its socioeconomic differences are stark. It stands among thirty countries in the world with the greatest gaps between rich and poor. The poorest 20 percent of the Dominican Republic's population make 3.3 percent of the country's income, while the richest 20 percent of the population make 52.1 percent of the country's income. The middle-earning 60 percent of the population make 44.6 percent of the country's income.

Most Dominicans live in poverty, while a smaller middle class struggles to stay out of poverty. An even smaller group composes a very rich upper class. About 42 percent of Dominicans are poor. They have incomes too low to meet their basic food and nonfood expenses. (Within this group, 16 percent of Dominicans are extremely poor. They have incomes too low to afford even their minimum food needs.) The remaining 58 percent of Dominicans make enough money to meet or exceed their basic expenses.

Luxury homes overlook the riverside shacks of the poor in Santo Domingo. Their residents' lifestyles could not be farther apart. Go to www.vgsbooks.com for links to more information about the health, education and welfare of the peoples of the Dominican Republic.

◉ Social Structure

For all Dominicans—regardless of ethnic or economic status—family is the basic social group. Parents teach their children that relatives must trust, help, and be loyal to each other. As a result, people tend to mistrust those outside their family circles.

Dominicans look to their families to understand where they fit in society. Family relationships show them not only where they can seek help but also where they must give help. In general, family members with better connections, more power, or higher income are expected to—and do—help less fortunate relatives.

Kinship also provides the foundation for formal organizations. Business partnerships and other public alliances work best when they mesh with existing family ties. Broad-based projects that involve entire communities or large interest groups tend to struggle, because they cross family boundaries.

Because family is so important in Dominican society, marriage is too. Marrying is a key way to extend or strengthen a family. Both religious and civil unions are socially acceptable. The upper class favors religious marriage, which is a sign of higher status. It usually involves a formal engagement followed by a church wedding and an elaborate fiesta (party). Religious marriage (and divorce) is difficult and expensive, so civil marriage (marriage performed by a judge) is common among the lower and middle classes.

Within a family, the father is typically an authority figure, and the mother is a nurturer. Males are the traditional breadwinners, but because poverty is so widespread in the Dominican Republic, many women add income-earning work to their traditional household duties. Parents teach their children gender roles beginning early in life, typically giving boys much more physical and behavioral freedom than they give girls.

◉ Education

The Dominican Republic requires children to attend six years of primary school. However, many Dominican children don't receive a full primary education. Few rural schools offer all six grades. And among the poor, many children must work to help their families survive. About 88 percent of children enroll in primary school. About 92 percent of children who attend primary school complete it. About 88 percent of children who attend primary school continue their education.

Students who finish primary school may attend any of various secondary schools. These secondary schools offer different types of education, such as university preparation, teacher training, techni-

Students attending this **school in a poor neighborhood in Santo Domingo** bring chairs from home every day if they can. Others sit on the dirt floor.

cal and scientific education, and vocational training. About 53 percent of children enroll in secondary school.

The Dominican Republic has a long history of higher education. The country is home to the oldest university in the New World, the Autonomous University of Santo Domingo (Universidad Autónoma de Santo Domingo or UASD), which began in 1538. Until the mid-1900s, UASD was the only local option available to Dominicans seeking college education. After Rafael Trujillo's death in 1961, Dominican higher education grew dramatically. By 2007 the nation had thirty-two public and private universities.

About 96 percent of the Dominican Republic's youth population can read and write. About 90 percent of the adult population can read and write.

These brothers are **hospitalized for mosquito-borne dengue fever** in Santo Domingo. More than two thousand cases are reported each year in the Dominican Republic.

▶ Health

Since the 1970s, campaigns to eliminate disease-causing insects, to improve sanitation, and to expand public health services into rural areas have improved overall Dominican health. Nevertheless, people in rural areas continue to have poorer health and less access to medical care than do people in urban areas.

The Dominican Republic's infant mortality rate is about thirty-one deaths per one thousand live births. This figure is better than the average Caribbean rate of forty deaths per one thousand live births. Dominican life expectancy at birth is sixty-nine years for females and sixty-six years for males. This figure is slightly worse than the average Caribbean expectancy of seventy-one years for females and sixty-seven years for males.

Among the Dominican Republic's health problems are high rates of tuberculosis (TB) and human immunodeficiency virus (HIV). The Dominican Republic has about ninety-one TB cases per one hundred thousand people. Its TB death rate is nineteen deaths per one hundred thousand people. With help from the international community, the Dominican Republic is working hard to reduce this rate.

About 1.1 percent of Dominican adults are infected with HIV, which causes acquired immunodeficiency syndrome (AIDS). This rate is about one-third that of Haiti, but Dominican programs for treating HIV lag far behind those of its poorer neighbor. About eight thousand Dominicans die of AIDS each year.

Visit www.vgsbooks.com for links to websites with detailed demographic information about the people of the Dominican Republic. Find out more about efforts to improve the Dominican school system and hospitals.

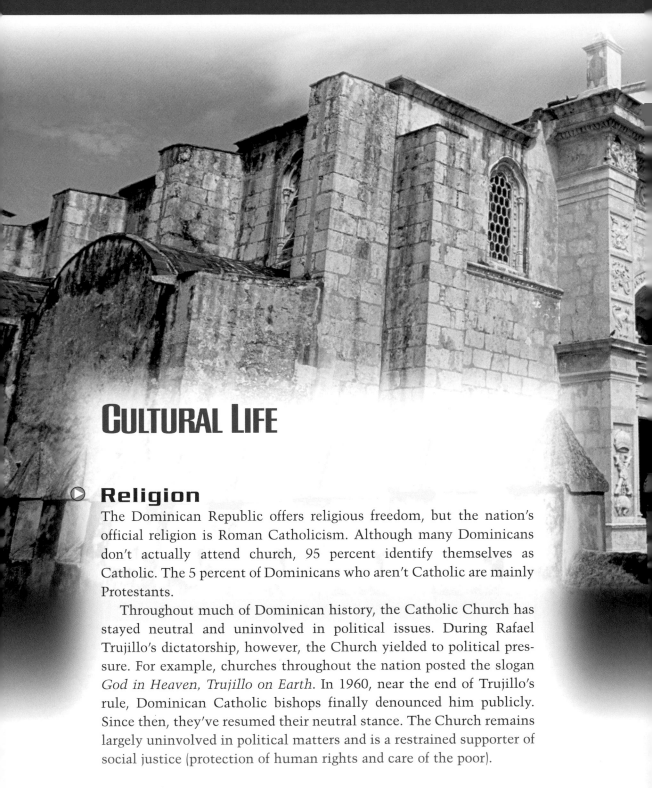

CULTURAL LIFE

Religion

The Dominican Republic offers religious freedom, but the nation's official religion is Roman Catholicism. Although many Dominicans don't actually attend church, 95 percent identify themselves as Catholic. The 5 percent of Dominicans who aren't Catholic are mainly Protestants.

Throughout much of Dominican history, the Catholic Church has stayed neutral and uninvolved in political issues. During Rafael Trujillo's dictatorship, however, the Church yielded to political pressure. For example, churches throughout the nation posted the slogan *God in Heaven, Trujillo on Earth*. In 1960, near the end of Trujillo's rule, Dominican Catholic bishops finally denounced him publicly. Since then, they've resumed their neutral stance. The Church remains largely uninvolved in political matters and is a restrained supporter of social justice (protection of human rights and care of the poor).

Most Dominicans of Haitian ancestry are Catholic but also practice voodoo, a folk religion whose believers honor family spirits. Voodooists believe their practices are consistent with Catholicism. Both Catholic and Protestant churches, however, condemn voodoo as pagan and evil.

Language

All Dominicans speak Spanish, the official language of the Dominican Republic. Dominican Spanish resembles other Latin American Spanish dialects, but it has some unique traits. Dominicans tend to drop the ends of words, particularly those ending in the letter s. Dominican Spanish also includes many Taino words, such as *mabi* (juice), *macana* (policeman's club), *macuto* (hand sack), and *chin-chin* (small amount).

Some Dominicans—especially those working in tourism—speak other European languages besides Spanish. English, French, German, and Italian are the main tourist languages. Haitian Dominicans generally speak Haitian Creole, a language based on French and some West African languages.

Literature

During the Spanish colonial period, Hispaniola was associated with two prominent writers. One of them was Bartolomé de las Casas. He was a Spanish friar who described Taino culture and Spanish abuses in *Brevísima relación de la destrucción de las Indias (A Brief Account of the Destruction of the Indies)*. De las Casas also recorded the early Spanish history in the Caribbean in *Historia de las Indias (History of the Indies)*. The other writer was Gabriel Téllez (also known as Tirso de Molina). He was a priest, poet, and playwright who helped reorganize the convent of Our Lady of Mercy in the city of Santo Domingo. This task formed the basis of his *Historia general de la Orden de la Mercéd* (General history of the Order of Mercy).

French literary style took center stage during the Haitian occupation from 1822 to 1844. During this period, many Dominican-born writers moved to other Spanish-speaking countries.

Dominican independence in 1844 sparked a national literary movement. Félix María del Monte is called the father of independent Dominican literature because he created the country's principal poetic form—a short patriotic poem based on local events of the day. Javier Angulo Guridi, Nicolás Ureña Mendoza, and José Joaquín Pérez were also literary leaders during the independence period.

Modern Dominican literature has developed through three main literary movements since the late nineteenth century. The *indigenismo* movement deals with the lives and problems of the Taino, often exaggerating their contributions to Dominican culture. One well-known indigenismo work is Manuel de Jesús Galván's 1882 novel *Enriquillo: Leyenda histórica dominicana* (Enriquillo: Dominican historical legend).

The *hispanidad* movement emphasized the Dominican Republic's white, Catholic, Spanish heritage. Both Trujillo's and Joaquín Balaguer's long regimes supported hispanidad. Works of this style view non-Catholics and nonwhites as inferiors. Balaguer, who was a prolific writer as well as a powerful leader, wrote two important hispanidad books: *Historia de la literatura dominicana* (History of Dominican literature) in Spanish and *Dominican Reality: Biographical Sketch of a Country and a Regime* in English.

The *criollismo* movement came to the forefront in the 1960s. Criollismo focused on the Dominican Republic's mixed Spanish and African culture. It opposed hispanidad as well as U.S. influence on Dominican culture. Juan Bosch, who was already a well-known short-story writer when he became president, was an important Dominican criollismo author. After he entered the political arena, he also earned praise for his nonfiction. After his overthrow, he wrote *The Unfinished Experiment: Democracy in the Dominican Republic*, which described his political life.

Many recent Dominican works of fiction highlight social themes. For example, the 1975 novel *Cañas y bueyes* (Sugarcane and Oxen) by Francisco Eugenio Moscoso Puello describes the sugar industry and its dominant role in the life of his country. Julia Álvarez's 1994 novel *In the Time of the Butterflies* dramatizes the story of the Mirabal sisters, who were assassinated in 1960 for their opposition to Trujillo. Dominican American Junot Díaz describes the modern Dominican immigrant experience in his acclaimed 1997 short-story collection *Drown*.

Music

Music is an important part of Dominican culture. Music and dance go hand in hand there. The country's two most popular styles of dance music are merengue and *bachata*. Both styles originated in the early 1900s. Each is a rich mixture of native, Spanish, and African influences. Dominicans generally view merengue as sophisticated urban music and bachata as lower-class country music.

Juan Luis Guerra is the best-known Dominican performer of both merengue and bachata. He and his band became famous for their merengue music. In 1990 they released a Grammy-award-winning album called *Bachata Rosa*, which brought merengue's country cousin into the international spotlight.

Children demonstrate the merengue in Puerto Plata, Dominican Republic. Find out more about Dominican music, dance, and the arts by going to www.vgsbooks.com for links.

Although merengue and bachata reign supreme in the Dominican Republic, the nation also embraces other musical styles, including classical, jazz, rock, and reggae. Dominicans organized a philharmonic society in 1855. During the rest of the nineteenth century, Dominican composers produced such widely different types of music as symphonies, choral works, and popular dance tunes. Alfredo Máximo Soler wrote more than three hundred popular compositions during his career.

Composers often use traditional dances, songs, and legends as the basis for serious music. In 1941 Dominicans established the National Conservatory of Music and Speech. Dominican composers contributed twenty important works that same year. In recent years, the collection and study of folk music has begun in earnest, with the encouragement of Edna Garrida. Garrida has compiled a volume of Dominican versions of traditional Spanish ballads.

◉ Visual Arts

The Dominican Republic began to develop a national visual art style in the late 1800s, after it gained independence from both Haiti and Spain. At this point, European trends began to mix with Dominican subjects such as religion, folklore, and African heritage. The nation hosted its first large exhibition of local artworks in 1890. It included landscapes, portraits, and copies of famous European works.

From 1920 to 1940, Dominican art embraced realism and neo-impressionism. Realistic art tried to represent nature accurately without idealizing it. Neo-impressionistic art tried to show the appearances of objects using thousands of tiny colored dots.

Trujillo's dictatorship from 1930 to 1961 strongly influenced Dominican visual art. Eager to put a positive face on his brutal regime, Trujillo poured money into cultural institutions. In 1942 he established the National School of Fine Arts. He also welcomed Spanish civil war refugees—including several well-known artists—who widened the horizons of young Dominican artists.

Trujillo's assassination in 1961 sparked a new era of social awareness in Dominican art. The nation's persistent social and political problems inspired Dominican artists to comment on current events and issues, such as immigration and prostitution.

Modern Dominican art follows a Caribbean trend of finding common ground instead of highlighting national differences. In 1992 Dominicans kicked off the Santo Domingo Biennial of Caribbean and Central American Painting. This event, which occurs every two years, gives regional artists exposure and a chance to network with each other.

Visit www.vgsbooks.com for links to websites with additional information about cultural life in the Dominican Republic. Listen to samples of merengue and bachata music, view pictures of Santo Domingo's famous Colonial Zone, and try Dominican recipes.

Architecture

The Dominican Republic's best-known structures are its Spanish colonial buildings. This type of architecture is very well preserved within the city of Santo Domingo's Colonial Zone. This large and well-preserved area is notable because it played a critical role in history. It served as the launchpad for most early European exploration of the New World. The zone is also the oldest continuously inhabited European settlement in the New World.

The United Nations Educational, Scientific, and Cultural Organization (UNESCO) has recognized Santo Domingo's importance by naming its entire Colonial Zone a UNESCO World Heritage site. This area contains (among many other structures) the New World's first hospital, first university, first two-story home, oldest working church, oldest monastery, and oldest surviving European fortress.

The Dominican Republic's colonial architecture is justly famous, but the nation is home to many other beautiful and culturally important architectural styles too. For example, both Santo Domingo and Santiago de los Caballeros sport Cuban Victorian, Caribbean Gingerbread, and Art Deco buildings. Both Puerto Plata (on the northern coast) and San Pedro de Macorís (on the southern coast) contain English and North American Victorian structures. And the entire country is sprinkled with colorful Antillean architecture.

The Dominican Republic's Taino heritage is evident in its rural buildings. For example, the Taino word *bohío* still describes a Dominican country house. Many Dominicans continue to build bohíos much like their Taino forebears did, in circular or rectangular shapes with cane roofs and walls made of palm fronds.

▶ Food

Dominicans take eating and drinking seriously, considering them important social activies. Families eat together whenever possible and can spend two hours over lunch. So many businesses close at midday and reopen in the afternoon. Breakfast, lunch, and dinner are all sizable, including a main dish and at least one side dish. Dominicans usually eat their biggest meal in the evening.

The Dominican diet's staples are eggs, meat, rice, beans, bananas and plantains, cassava, seafood, and a wide variety of fruits and vegetables. Poorer Dominicans often eat rice, beans, and soup, only sometimes indulging in meat and fish. The most common Dominican meal (usually eaten for lunch) is *la bandera* (the flag), which mirrors the nation's flag colors with white rice, red beans, and stewed meat or fish. Other common foods are mashed, boiled bananas or plantains and a bread called *casabe*, which is made from cassava flour.

For special occasions, Dominicans treasure *sancocho de siete carnes*, a stew made with seven kinds of meat and various vegetables. *Sopa criolla dominicana* (Dominican Creole soup) is another popular dish. It contains stew meat, carrots, peppercorns, vermicelli (thin spaghetti), onions, potatoes, cabbage, and herbs. *Pastelón de vegetables* (baked vegetable cake) is a rich mixture of green beans, carrots, eggs, cheese, peas, cabbage, beets, onions, tomatoes, pickles, and spices.

The Dominican Republic's signature beverages take advantage of the country's plentiful fruit and sugarcane. Dominicans make *batidas* (smoothies) with crushed fruit, water, ice, sugar, and sometimes milk. Fresh-squeezed *jugos* (juices) made from tropical fruits such as pineapple, passion fruit, tamarind, and orange are popular too. Local adults also

MORIR SOÑANDO

Some Dominican batidas have unusual names. *Morir soñando*, for example, means "to die dreaming." This cool, refreshing smoothie is great for a quick energy boost.

4 cups evaporated milk

½ cup sugar

2½ cups ice cubes

2 cups orange juice

1. Mix the milk and sugar in a pitcher until the sugar dissolves. Place the pitcher in the freezer until the mixture is very cold but not frozen.
2. Remove the pitcher from the freezer and add the ice to the milk-sugar mixture.
3. Slowly pour in the orange juice, stirring constantly.
4. Serve immediately.

Serves 4.

enjoy Dominican rum (an alcohol made from molasses, a by-product of sugarcane processing), which is famous for its high quality.

▶ Sports and Recreation

In the Dominican Republic, the only team sport with a truly national following is baseball. The nation has six professional teams of its own, and Dominicans are devoted fans of U.S. and Caribbean major league teams. Dominican athletes are valuable players on many U.S. baseball

Playing U.S. major league baseball for the Texas Rangers, Dominican Sammy Sosa excited his fans on June 20, 2007, by hitting his six-hundredth home run against the Chicago Cubs.

teams. Moreover, the Dominican Republic is the hub of Caribbean baseball competition, which takes place each winter after the North American World Series.

Volleyball and basketball are popular too, and soccer has an active—though small—following. For wealthy people, clubs provide opportunities to sail, water-ski, windsurf, and play polo and tennis.

In 1974 Santo Domingo was the scene of the Twelfth Central American and Caribbean Olympic Games, in which about four thousand athletes participated. For the event, Dominican authorities built a large sports palace with seating capacity for ten thousand spectators, an Olympic-size swimming pool, a bicycle track, a shooting range, and facilities and fields for a wide variety of competitions.

In the Dominican Republic, one additional sport—cockfighting—is just as popular as baseball. Nearly every town and city has a *gallero* (cockfighting ring). All social classes participate. At cockfights, carefully bred roosters equipped with metal spikes duel each other to the death. Meanwhile, spectators bet on the fights. Many foreigners find this sport cruel, but it has a long history among Dominicans. It's such an important part of the culture that many national organizations use the fighting rooster as their symbol.

◉ Holidays and Festivals

Because it's a strongly Catholic country, the Dominican Republic's calendar of holidays includes many religious ones. Dominicans also celebrate a few important secular dates.

To usher in New Year's Day (January 1), some Dominicans practice good-luck rituals. For example, they may thoroughly clean the house, being careful to put away all cleaning gear before midnight on New Year's Eve to prevent the New Year from sweeping away the good with the bad. They may also leave doors and windows open to let the spirit of the past exit. Another good-luck tradition is eating twelve grapes at midnight. With each clock chime, people eat one grape and make one wish. Still another custom is wearing the lucky colors navy blue, yellow, green, and white.

The feast day of Our Lady of Altagracia (January 21) is the Dominican Republic's most important religious holiday besides Christmas. Our Lady of Altagracia (a name for Mary, the mother of Jesus) is the Dominican Republic's patron saint. She's believed to have performed a miracle in the southeastern town of Higüey. Each year thousands of Catholic pilgrims visit Higüey's cathedral to honor her on her feast day. The word *Altagracia* means "high grace."

Carnaval is an extended party complete with parades and costumes. It happens around the country every weekend of February. It ends with

Carnaval in Santo Domingo features parades of people in costume. These people are dressed as roosters.

a huge bash on Independence Day (February 27). Carnaval began as a colonial Catholic tradition influenced by African slaves. But in the modern Dominican Republic, Carnaval has more to do with Independence Day than Catholicism. Independence Day marks the day in 1844 when the Dominican Republic gained freedom from Haitian rule.

The feast day of the Virgin of Mercedes (September 24) is another important religious holiday that honors Mary, the mother of Jesus. The Virgin of Mercedes is Hispaniola's patron saint. She's believed to have performed a miracle in the city of Santo Domingo. The word *Mercedes* means "blessings."

At the **Carnaval parades in the town of La Vega**, revelers are famous for whacking each other—as well as innocent bystanders—on the backside with *vejigas* (reinforced cow or pig bladders).

Christmas (December 25) is the Dominican Republic's most important religious holiday. Celebrations start early in December. Most employees receive a Christmas bonus of one month's salary during this time. Family and friends share a special dinner (which often includes sancocho) on Christmas Eve. Diners may be visited by musicians singing and playing *aguinaldos* (carols). Many Dominicans attend church services at midnight on Christmas Eve or at midday on Christmas Day. Some exchange gifts on Christmas Day. Most people wait to do so until the end of the Christmas season, the feast of the Epiphany (January 6).

THE ECONOMY

During the 1970s, the Dominican Republic's government and private sector began working together to change the nation's one-crop economy. Relying heavily on sugarcane farming and processing had put the country at the mercy of constantly rising and falling sugar prices.

Programs to develop more manufacturing, tourism, and a wider range of crops have paid off. In 1985 tourism earned more income (440 million dollars) than sugar did for the first time in Dominican history. In 1994 tourism earnings reached 1.26 billion dollars. By 2005 the service sector, which includes tourism, banking, and other businesses that don't produce material goods, was by far the largest sector of the economy. Industry was the second largest, and agriculture was the smallest.

Although the Dominican Republic has worked hard to stabilize its economy by varying its income sources, the past few decades have had their ups and downs. After a stagnant 1980s, the Dominican Republic's economy boomed in the 1990s. From 1996 to 2000, its

growth rate was the highest in Latin America. The economy shrank dramatically after September 11, 2001. In 2003 the country's three biggest private banks collapsed. The government bailed out the banks' depositors, a move that caused a massive fiscal shortfall. This shortfall led to inflation, currency devaluation, and higher taxes. By 2005 the economy was on the road to recovery.

Services

The Dominican Republic's service sector includes commerce, transportation, telecommunications, hotels, bars, restaurants, financial services, housing, and government services. In 2005 this sector was responsible for 58 percent of the nation's gross domestic product (GDP). (GDP is the total value of goods and services produced inside the country.)

Tourism is the most important Dominican service business. It's also the leading earner of income from other nations. Dominican

This resort hotel is in **Punta Cana,** one of the Dominican Republic's top tourist destinations. Go to www.vgsbooks.com for more information about tourism in the Dominican Republic.

tourism has grown dramatically during the last four decades. During the 1970s, tourism accounted for less than 1 percent of the GDP. Since the mid-1990s, it has accounted for 6 to 7 percent of GDP. From 1970 to 2004, tourism grew an average of 14 percent per year. Even while the rest of the economy slumped from 2000 to 2004, tourism grew an average of over 6 percent per year. The currency devaluation that harmed other sectors of the economy helped tourism by making the Dominican Republic a cheap destination for foreigners. In this way, tourism helped cushion the overall impact of the 2003 banking crisis.

Other types of services, including construction, transportation, commerce, utilities, and government services, also grew—but more slowly—from 1970 to 2004. For example, the booming tourism industry caused an explosion in construction of new hotels and infrastructure (public works such as roads, phone lines, electrical service, and sanitation). Private companies have kept pace with the demand for hotels, bars, restaurants, and other new buildings, but the government has struggled to provide adequate infrastructure—with uneven results.

The Dominican Republic's transportation infrastructure, for example, is well developed. Five main highways connect its major cities and tourist centers. It has about 7,830 miles (12,600 km) of roads in total. About 3,870 miles (6,228 km) of these roads are paved. The country also has about 470 miles (756 km) of railways. It has eight large seaports and several smaller ones along its coast. It has twenty-nine airports, thirteen with paved runways and seven with international service.

The Dominican Republic's energy infrastructure, on the other hand, is inadequate. The nation's energy resources are limited. Though it has some coal and oil reserves, it doesn't extract these fuels. Several of the country's rivers have hydroelectric dams, but these supply only a small fraction of the nation's energy. Instead, the Dominican Republic relies heavily on imported oil to generate power. But power supply often falls short of demand. Dominicans endure frequent power outages that last from a couple of hours to more than twelve hours per day. Electricity theft, nonpayment from customers, and delayed government subsidy (grant money) payments are the main culprits. High oil prices and an inefficient system magnify the problem. The electricity crisis has a huge negative impact on the economy. Many businesses must generate their own electricity to ensure safe and smooth operations, which is very expensive.

The Dominican Republic's ongoing electricity crisis and its 2003 banking crisis are two examples of problems caused by the country's weak economic governance. The government's economic activities are often corrupt, secretive, costly, and ineffective. As a result, the public has low confidence in government services and low respect for business laws. Weak governance hinders the economy by discouraging honest investment, misusing public resources, signaling that laws aren't binding, and discouraging tax payment. Tax evasion leads to underfunding, which leads to new taxes. New taxes raise both the cost of doing business and the temptation to evade taxes, fueling a vicious cycle of economic problems.

◗ Industry

The Dominican Republic's industrial sector includes manufacturing and mining. In 2005 this sector was responsible for 31 percent of the nation's GDP. Since the 1970s, the Dominican Republic has greatly increased its production of consumer goods and the output of its chemical, metal, beverage, and food-processing plants.

To stimulate manufacturing growth and encourage foreign investment, Dominican authorities created free trade zones (FTZs). In these zones, companies get large tax breaks in exchange for building new factories or for expanding existing ones that produce goods for export (sale to other countries). In addition to tax breaks, the government offers advice on the potential for new industries and on the availability of local workers.

Thousands of Dominicans operate small businesses either in their homes or in vacant spaces. Mechanics, for example, maintain full-service garages on quiet residential streets. Home-based manufacturers produce furniture, clothing, shoes, and machine parts. The whir of sewing machines, the buzz of table saws, and the clatter of trucks loading and unloading are familiar noises during the day in even the poorest Dominican neighborhoods.

The Dominican Republic has had FTZs since the 1950s, but they didn't become a driving force in the nation's manufacturing until the late 1980s. Between 1985 and 2004, the number of FTZs increased from three to fifty-eight, and the number of firms jumped from 136 to 569. During the same period, employment in FTZs grew from 31,000 to 190,000 people. The value of exports increased from 215 million to 4.7 billion dollars, accounting for about 80 percent of all Dominican goods exports and half of all Dominican goods and services exports. Within the FTZs, both local and foreign companies produce everything from clothing to pleasure boats to processed food products.

Mining accounts for only a small portion of the Dominican Republic's industry. It is a tiny portion of the nation's overall economy. Though Dominican mining is relatively unimportant, the nation does extract and process a variety of mineral resources, including bauxite, cement, nickel, gypsum, limestone, marble, salt, sand and gravel, and steel. It also has deposits of gold, silver, zinc, copper, and amber.

Agriculture

The Dominican Republic's agricultural sector includes farming, fishing, and forestry. In 2005 this sector was responsible for 11 percent of the nation's GDP. The Dominican economy has become less and less dependent on agriculture during the past four decades as industry has taken its place.

A Haitian cuts sugarcane with a machete (large heavy knife) on a plantation in the Dominican Republic. Most Haitians are low-paid laborers and work in agriculture. Regardless of where they work, Haitians face discrimination. Those working in the country illegally also face deportation.

Unlike most other Caribbean countries, the Dominican Republic produces most of its own food. It also exports a large amount of food. Sugarcane remains the main cash crop. But as sugar prices fell during the twentieth century, other crops became more important. These crops include coffee, cacao, tobacco, rice, tomatoes, vegetables, bananas and other tropical fruits, root crops, and sorghum. Booming tourism has raised demand for—and production of—chickens, eggs, pork, beef, and dairy products.

CANE CUTTING

Sugarcane harvesting has changed little since the 1870s, when sugar became big business in the Dominican Republic. On most plantations, workers stretch and bend for about twelve hours per day in the tropical sun, cutting down the cane, stripping off the leaves, chopping it into small pieces, and piling it up. They wear no protective gear and must buy their own machetes (large, heavy knives). Bosses on horseback check their progress. Tractors drive up every few hours to haul away the cut cane. The average cane cutter earns $2.50 per day.

Laundry dries on **a clothesline over a cabbage field** in the central Dominican Republic.

Cropland ownership is concentrated in the hands of a traditional, conservative Dominican aristocracy (small group of upper-class families). These farmers usually own huge plantations and can afford good machinery and seeds, as well as many workers. Small farms struggle to survive. Their owners often must supplement their incomes by selling handicrafts such as baskets, pottery, rocking chairs, and straw hats.

The Dominican Republic's fish supply is plentiful enough to meet local needs, and sport fishing is a tourist attraction. However, because marketable fish are scarce in nearby waters and because the government offers little financial or other assistance for commercial fishing, the nation has no large-scale fishing industry. Its fishing industry consists of small coastal fishing families with small, nonrefrigerated boats.

Many valuable trees—including mahogany, lignum vitae, satinwood, juniper, and pine—are native to Hispaniola. However, logging and agriculture have destroyed most of the Dominican Republic's native forest. (Experts estimate native forest loss of up to 90 percent.) To offset this deforestation, the government outlawed commercial logging in 1967. Since then, the nation has developed some small tree plantations. But forestry has little impact on the economy. The Dominican Republic continues to import most of the wood products it needs.

Foreign Trade

The Dominican Republic's most important trading partner is the United States. About 75 percent of Dominican export income comes from the United States. The other 25 percent comes from Canada, western Europe, and Japan. The Dominican Republic exports FTZ-manufactured products as well as nickel, sugar, coffee, cacao, and tobacco. The country imports oil, industrial raw materials, and food. It imports more goods than it exports.

On September 5, 2005, the Dominican congress approved a trade agreement with the United States and five Central American countries

Dominican exports include its people. Almost one million Dominican citizens live abroad, mainly in the United States. They send home about one billion U.S. dollars per year.

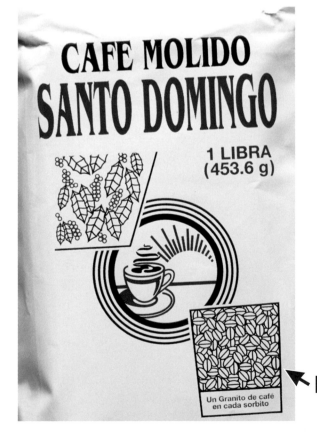

CAFE MOLIDO
SANTO DOMINGO
1 LIBRA
(453.6 g)
Un Granito de café en cada sorbito

Coffee is one of the Dominican Republic's more recent export crops.

Leaders who signed the CAFTA-DR agreement in 2005 include *(left to right)* **President Leonel Fernandez Reyna of the Dominican Republic, President Óscar Berger Perdomo of Guatemala, President Enrique Bolaños Geyer of Nicaragua, U.S. president George W. Bush, President Abel de Jesus Pacheco de la Espriella of Costa Rica, President Elías Antonio Saca González of El Salvador, and Vice President Alberto Díaz Lobo of Honduras.**

(Costa Rica, El Salvador, Guatemala, Honduras, and Nicaragua). This agreement is called the Central America–Dominican Republic–United States Free Trade Agreement (CAFTA-DR). CAFTA-DR took effect in the Dominican Republic on March 1, 2007. Among many other provisions, it drastically reduces Dominican taxes on goods imported from the United States.

Drug Trafficking

In the early twenty-first century, the Dominican Republic (along with its neighbor, Haiti) have experienced an alarming surge in drug trafficking. A convenient location, government corruption, weak legal systems, and hundreds of miles of open borders and coastline have converted the island of Hispaniola into a drug-trafficking haven.

While there is a growing amount of drug use on the island, the Dominican Republic and Haiti are mainly stopovers for drugs traveling from South America to North America and Europe. The rise in trafficking has prompted numerous drug busts. However, both the Dominican Republic and Haiti have a chronic lack of funds, personnel, training, and a master strategy to cope with the larger problem.

Visit www.vgsbooks.com for links to websites with more information about the economy of the Dominican Republic. Get the latest business news, find currency conversion rates, and read about efforts to decrease foreign debt.

The Future

The early twenty-first century proved to be a difficult time for many Dominicans, as crises such as inflation and unemployment ravaged their country's economy. Although the Dominican government is continuing public-works programs and taking steps to increase foreign investment while reducing foreign debt, the country is still dependent on foreign aid and loans. Unrest among urban workers, whose wages are not keeping up with rising prices, threatens the stability of President Fernandez's government.

Nevertheless, the Dominican Republic has broken its historic cycle of dependency, tyranny, and underdevelopment. The last forty years of peaceful self-government may not have brought great material advantages, but they have rekindled Dominican initiative and have prepared the nation for the struggles of the future.

Dominican students pose for a group photo at the San Diego gate in Santo Domingo. Catch up on the latest news about the Dominican Republic. Go to www.vgsbooks.com for news links.

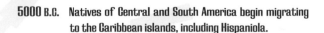

Timeline

5000 B.C. Natives of Central and South America begin migrating to the Caribbean islands, including Hispaniola.

A.D. 1000 Hispaniola has a well-developed Taino culture.

LATE 1400s The five Taino groups on Hispaniola are on the verge of unifying.

1492 Sailing westward from Spain in hopes of reaching Asia, Christopher Columbus lands on Hispaniola.

1493 Columbus builds a fort on Hispaniola called La Navidad.

1494 Columbus establishes a second settlement on Hispaniola called La Isabela.

LATE 1490s Columbus's brother Bartholomew founds the cities of Santo Domingo and Santiago de los Caballeros. The Spaniards call their new colony Santo Domingo.

EARLY 1500s Santo Domingo serves as the key base from which Spain extends its empire in the New World. Taino society is eliminated.

1519 Taino cacique Enriquillo begins a rebellion that lasts about fifteen years.

1538 Colonists establish the New World's first university.

MID-1500s Santo Domingo begins to struggle as Spain's priorities shift westward.

1605 Spain forcibly relocates the residents of northern and western Hispaniola to settlements near the city of Santo Domingo.

1600s The relocation impoverishes the entire colony and makes much of its land vulnerable.

1697 Spain signs the Treaty of Ryswick, ceding the western third of Hispaniola (renamed Saint-Domingue) to France.

1795 Spain signs the Treaty of Basel, yielding the remaining colony of Santo Domingo to France.

1804 Saint-Domingue declares its independence from France and renames itself Haiti.

1809 Spanish colonists in Santo Domingo throw out the French. Santo Domingo reverts to Spain.

1821 Santo Domingo secedes from Spain.

1822 Haiti takes over Santo Domingo.

1844 The Dominican Republic secedes from Haiti.

1861 Spain annexes the Dominican Republic, making it a colony again.

1865 Spain withdraws from the Dominican Republic.

1882 Military dictator Ulises Heureaux becomes president.

1888 Dutch banking firm Westendorp begins managing Dominican customs.

1893   The U.S.-based San Domingo Improvement Company (SDIC) takes over Dominican customs.

1899   Rebels assassinate Heureaux.

1901   The Dominican Republic kicks out SDIC for mismanagement.

1905   The U.S. government takes over Dominican finances.

1916   The U.S. Marine Corps takes control of the Dominican government.

1924   The marines leave the Dominican Republic.

1930   Military dictator Rafael Trujillo seizes power from president Horacio Vásquez.

1950s The mostly rural Dominican population begins to shift to urban areas.

1960   Trujillo orders the murder of the Mirabal sisters. He also tries to have Venezuelan president Rómulo Betancourt assassinated.

1961   Trujillo is assassinated.

1965   In April, civil war erupts in Santo Domingo, and foreign troops intervene. The war ruins Santo Domingo and kills about four thousand people before ending in August.

1966   Foreign troops withdraw. Joaquin Balaguer wins the presidency and begins an intermittent thirty-year regime.

1967   To offset deforestation, the Dominican government outlaws commercial logging.

1970s Worldwide recession and low sugar prices devastate the Dominican economy. The government starts intensively developing tourism and manufacturing.

1980s Scholars begin to question the widely held concept of Taino extinction.

1994   Balaguer wins the presidency dishonestly, which forces him to shorten his term. This election inspires major changes in the Dominican constitution.

1996   Balaguer steps down. Leonel Fernández begins the first of two terms.

1998   Hurricane Georges causes widespread destruction and death.

2003   The Dominican Republic's three biggest banks collapse, causing an economic crash.

2004   The Solie River floods, displacing and killing thousands of Dominicans and Haitians.

2005   The Dominican congress approves the Central America-Dominican Republic–United States Free Trade Agreement (CAFTA-DR).

2006   Bajos de Haina is named one of the world's ten most polluted cities.

2007   CAFTA-DR takes effect. Fernández announces his plan to run for a third term.

Currency Fast Facts

COUNTRY NAME Dominican Republic

AREA 18,815 square miles (48,730 square km)

MAIN LANDFORMS Cordillera Central, Cordillera Septentrional, Sierra de Neiba, Sierra de Baoruco, Cordillera Oriental, Cibao Valley, coastal plains

HIGHEST POINT Pico Duarte, 10,164 feet (3,098 m) above sea level

LOWEST POINT Lake Enriquillo, 131 feet (40 m) below sea level

MAJOR RIVERS Camú River, Yaque del Norte, Yaque del Sur, Yuna River

ANIMALS American crocodiles, dolphins, frigate birds, Hispaniolan lizard-cuckoos, humpback whales, hutias, Jaragua lizards, manatees, mongooses, parrots, rhinoceros iguanas, roseate spoonbills, sea turtles, solenodons

CAPITAL CITY Santo Domingo

OTHER MAJOR CITIES Santiago de los Caballeros

OFFICIAL LANGUAGE Spanish

MONETARY UNIT Dominican peso. 100 centavos = 1 peso.

CURRENCY

The Dominican Republic's currency is the Dominican peso, also called the *peso oro*. Its international currency code is DOP, and its written symbol is RD$. The government introduced the peso oro in 1937 to replace the U.S. currency in circulation at the time. Coins come in denominations of 1, 5, 10, 25, and 50 centavos (¢) and 1, 5, 10, and 25 pesos. (Coins below 50 centavos are rare.) Paper notes come in denominations of 10, 20, 50, 100, 500, 1000, and 2000 pesos.

The Dominican Republic adopted its flag in November 1844, after gaining independence from Haiti earlier that year. The Dominican flag has its roots in the Haitian flag of the early 1800s.

The flag consists of a centered white cross that extends to the edges. The cross divides the flag into four rectangles. On the top half of the flag, the left rectangle is blue, and the right one is red. On the bottom half, the left rectangle is red, and the right one is blue. The state flag, flown on government buildings, includes a small coat of arms at the center of the cross. This emblem shows a shield supported by an olive branch (left) and a palm branch (right). Above the shield a blue ribbon displays the motto *DIOS, PATRIA, LIBERTAD* (God, nation, liberty). Below the shield, the words REPUBLICA DOMINICANA (Dominican Republic) appear on a red ribbon.

"Quisqueyanos Valientes" ("Valiant Sons of Quisqueya") is the national anthem of the Dominican Republic. Jose Reyes (1835–1905) composed the melody, and his friend Emilio Prud'homme (1856–1932) wrote the lyrics. The anthem's first public performance took place on August 17, 1883.

The song quickly grew popular. In 1897 the Dominican congress approved it as the nation's official anthem, but President Heureaux refused to sign the act. In 1934, many years after Heureaux's death, President Trujillo adopted the song as the national anthem. The first verse of the Dominican anthem appears below.

Valiant Sons of Quisqueya

Brave men of Quisqueya,
Let us sing with strong feeling
And let us show to the world
Our invincible, glorious banner.

Visit www.vgsbooks.com for a link to a website where you can hear the melody of the Dominican Republic's national anthem.

Famous People

JOAQUÍN BALAGUER (1906–2002) Balaguer, a lawyer and writer, served six terms as president of the Dominican Republic between 1960 and 1996. He was born in Villa Bisonó (later renamed Navarrette). He became a professor of law at the Autonomous University of Santo Domingo in 1938. He also held high positions in Trujillo's dictatorial government (1930–1961). After Trujillo's assassination, Balaguer fled to the United States, but he returned in 1965 to begin a long political regime. Charges of election fraud forced him to step down in 1996 from his final presidential term. He died of heart failure in Santo Domingo.

JUAN BOSCH (1909–2001) Bosch was a scholar, poet, and president of the Dominican Republic. He was born in La Vega and raised in a working-class family. He became a vocal critic of Trujillo and fled the country in 1938. He returned after Trujillo's death, won the presidency, and began major reforms as soon as he took office in 1963, but was overthrown by the military a few months later. When his supporters revolted, the United States sent in troops to suppress them, claiming they were Communists. Over the next three decades, Bosch ran repeatedly but unsuccessfully for president. He died in Santo Domingo.

CHRISTOPHER COLUMBUS (1451–1506) Columbus launched Europe's conquest of the Americas. He was born to Spanish parents in Genoa, Italy. In 1492 he persuaded Spain to sponsor a westward voyage to Asia. On his first voyage (1492–1493), he landed on Hispaniola and built a fort there. On his second voyage (1493–1496), he founded La Isabela, the first European town in the New World. Reports of his incompetence as ruler of Santo Domingo led to his replacement and arrest. The Spanish monarchy pardoned him, but he never regained his former honor. He died of a heart attack in Valladolid, Spain. History remembers him as a brilliant navigator and zealous Christian but also vain, greedy, and cruel.

JUAN PABLO DUARTE (1813–1876) Duarte is considered the father of Dominican independence. He was born in Santo Domingo and left to study in Spain after the colony came under Haitian rule. When he returned, he and several other patriots organized a secret society called La Trinitaria to work toward independence. His first attempt to oust the Haitians in 1843 collapsed, and he fled the country, but his followers succeeded the next year. In 1844 Duarte returned, and the Dominican Republic proclaimed its independence. However, military strongman Pedro Santana forced Duarte into exile again. He moved to Venezuela and spent the rest of his life there.

ENRIQUILLO (1500s–1530s) Enriquillo was a Taino cacique who led a rebellion against the Spaniards from 1519 to the mid-1530s. He was born on the southern coast of Hispaniola into an important Taino family. After his father's death, Catholic priests raised Enriquillo in a Santo Domingo monastery; he eventually returned as a cacique to his native village. When colonial authorities refused to punish a Spaniard who had raped Enriquillo's wife and threatened to imprison Enriquillo for complaining, he fled to the mountains. There he organized an independent Taino settlement and resisted the Spaniards for more than a dozen years. In the mid-1530s, the Spanish finally signed a treaty with Enriquillo, allowing his community to live in peace. Enriquillo died the following year, and the Spaniards broke the agreement a few years later.

LEONEL FERNÁNDEZ (b. 1953) Fernández is a Dominican lawyer and president. He was born in Santo Domingo and spent his childhood in New York City. He returned home to earn a law degree at the Autonomous University of Santo Domingo. He served as president from 1996 to 2000 and from 2004 to 2008. His government focused on economic reform, technological development, and international participation.

JUAN LUIS GUERRA (b. 1957) Guerra is an internationally acclaimed popular musician. He was born in Santo Domingo. After graduating from the National Conservatory of Music and Speech in Santo Domingo, he studied composition at the Berklee College of Music in Boston, Massachusetts. He returned home, and with his band, 440, released his first album in 1984. In 1990 Guerra and 440 earned their first Grammy Award for the album *Bachata Rosa*. Guerra's music encompasses merengue, bachata, rock, gospel, and many other contemporary styles. He is known for bringing international attention to merengue and bachata.

ANTONIA MARÍA TERESA MIRABAL (1935–1960), **MARIA ARGENTINA MINERVA MIRABAL** (1926–1960), and **PATRIA MERCEDES MIRABAL** (1924–1960) The Mirabal sisters were political activists assassinated by Trujillo. They were born in the city of Salcedo to a wealthy, aristocratic family that lost its fortune when Trujillo took power. Together they formed an anti-Trujillo movement, within which they were known as the Butterflies. Trujillo imprisoned and tortured them and their husbands several times, but they continued their fight to end his dictatorship. Finally, on November 25, 1960, he ordered his men to murder the sisters. Their deaths caused a public outrage that eventually led to Trujillo's own assassination in 1961. Dominicans honor the anniversary of their deaths, and Julia Álvarez honors their lives in her novel *In the Time of the Butterflies*.

RAFAEL TRUJILLO (1891–1961) Trujillo was a notorious twentieth-century Dominican dictator. He was born in San Cristóbal to a lower-class family and entered the army in 1918. He rose quickly through the ranks and became a general in 1927. In 1930 he seized power from president Horacio Vásquez. He stayed in absolute control until he was assassinated in 1961. Though the country seemed to prosper under Trujillo, the new wealth flowed straight to his family and friends. Most Dominicans suffered poverty and repression during his rule. History remembers Trujillo as extraordinarily vain, corrupt, and cruel.

AMBER MUSEUMS The Dominican Republic is home to two amber museums: the Amber Museum in Puerto Plata and the Amber World Museum in Santo Domingo. Both have large collections of high-quality amber specimens, many containing preserved prehistoric plants and animals.

BASILICA OF OUR LADY OF ALTAGRACIA Dominicans built this church during the 1970s in Higüey to honor their patron saint, who is believed to have performed a miracle there. Each year on January 21, thousands of Catholic pilgrims visit the church.

COLONIAL ZONE OF SANTO DOMINGO The oldest section of the Dominican Republic's capital city served as the launchpad for early European exploration of the New World. It's also the oldest continuously inhabited European settlement in the New World. It contains the New World's first hospital, first university, first paved road, first two-story home, oldest working church, oldest monastery, and oldest surviving European fortress.

COLUMBUS LIGHTHOUSE Joaquín Balaguer's government completed this Santo Domingo monument in 1992, just in time to mark the five hundredth anniversary of Christopher Columbus's arrival in the Americas. The enormous cross-shaped building houses Columbus's tomb, as well as several museums and galleries. At night, 157 lights on its roof project a cross into the sky.

LAKE ENRIQUILLO This extremely salty lake near the Haitian border is the largest inland body of water in the Caribbean and is also the lowest location in the Caribbean. It hosts one of the biggest known populations of American crocodiles, as well as other rare animals, such as rhinoceros iguanas.

MIRABAL SISTERS MUSEUM Bélgica Adela Mirabal-Reyes, sibling of the assassinated Mirabal sisters, operates this museum in Salcedo to keep the women's story alive. Housed on the Mirabal family property, the museum includes personal items, artifacts from the murder, and the sisters' graves.

MUSEUM OF THE DOMINICAN MAN This museum is located in Santo Domingo. It traces the country's cultural evolution from the Taino to the present through a variety of pre-Columbian artifacts, Spanish colonial artifacts, items related to the slave trade, and more.

PICO DUARTE The Dominican Republic's highest mountain is accessible from two of the country's eleven national parks: Armando Bermudez National Park and Jose del Carmen National Park. Both parks are popular destinations for backpackers.

cacique: a native chief in Latin America

caudillo: a Latin American military dictator. A caudillo is usually a man with a magnetic personality whose power depends on personal relationships, violence, armed followers, favors and bribes, and constant watchfulness.

Communist: someone who supports a political system in which people own all property collectively

conservative: someone whose political philosophy is based on a belief in tradition, social stability, established institutions, and gradual change

currency devaluation: a drop in the value of one currency compared to other currencies

customs: taxes collected by a government on goods imported into the country or exported out of it

democracy: a form of government in which the people exercise power directly (by voting on issues) or indirectly (through freely elected representatives who vote on the people's behalf)

dictatorship: a form of government in which one ruler or a very small group of rulers has absolute power

fraud: cheating to gain something valuable, such as money or votes

genocide: mass murder in order to destroy a specific racial, political, or cultural group

inflation: a persistent rise in prices

liberal: someone whose political philosophy is based on a belief in progress, the essential goodness of humans, and the importance of personal freedom

Glossary

Atkins, G. Pope. *The Dominican Republic and the United States: From Imperialism to Transnationalism.* Athens, GA: University of Georgia Press, 1998.

This book explains U.S.-Dominican relations from their colonial eras to the late 1900s. It shows how international powers strongly influenced Dominican history, with special attention to the twentieth century.

Caribbean Journal of Science. June 2007.
http://caribjsci.org (September 12, 2007)

This peer-reviewed print and online journal publishes articles, research notes, and book reviews on Caribbean botany, zoology, ecology, conservation biology and management, geology, archaeology, and paleontology.

Castro, Max, Christine Mataya, and Jeffrey Stark. *Environmental Security in the Dominican Republic: Promise or Peril?* Falls Church, VA: Foundation for Environmental Security and Sustainability, 2005.
http://www.fess-global.org/files/dr_esaf_full_report.pdf (September 12, 2007)

This report assesses the status and future of the environment in the Dominican Republic. It highlights the connection between societal security and the use of natural resources.

Dominican Republic Country Economic Memorandum: The Foundations of Growth and Competitiveness. September 2006.
http://siteresources.worldbank.org/INTLAC/Resources/257803-1163791621413/FINALDRCEM.pdf (September 12, 2007)

This comprehensive report, a joint effort of the World Bank and the Dominican government, closely analyzes the Dominican Republic's recent economic history and its future potential.

Dominican Republic Poverty Assessment: Achieving More Pro-Poor Growth. October 30, 2006.
http://iris37.worldbank.org/domdoc/PRD/Other/PRDDContainer.nsf/WB_ViewAttachments?ReadForm&ID=85256D2400766CC7852572890074BCA1& (September 12, 2007)

This report explores the trends and causes of poverty in the Dominican Republic. It also recommends economic and social policies to help reduce Dominican poverty.

FAO Country Profiles and Mapping Information System: Dominican Republic. 2007.
http://www.fao.org/countryprofiles/index.asp?lang=en&iso3=DOM (September 12, 2007)

This website links readers to detailed articles and maps describing the environment, economy, agriculture, forestry, and fishing of the Dominican Republic.

Kacike: Journal of Caribbean Amerindian History and Anthropology. April 12, 2007.
http://www.kacike.org (September 12, 2007)

This online, peer-reviewed journal publishes academic articles, reports, and reviews on native Caribbean societies and communities in the past and present.

Metz, Helen Chapin. *Dominican Republic and Haiti: Country Studies.* Washington, DC: U.S. Government Printing Office, 2001.

This is a comprehensive handbook on the Dominican Republic and Haiti that gives background on both countries' geography, climate, history, economy, society, political affairs, and culture.

Selected Bibliography

Moya Pons, Frank. *The Dominican Republic: A National History.* **Princeton, NJ: Markus Wiener Publishers, 1998.**
This book examines the economic, political, social, and cultural history of the Dominican Republic. It spans from the settlement of Hispaniola by native immigrants from South America thousands of years ago to the end of the twentieth century.

Pacini Hernandez, Deborah. *Bachata: A Social History of a Dominican Popular Music.* **Philadelphia: Temple University Press, 1995.**
This book traces the development of bachata and the Dominican music industry, offering a unique perspective on five decades of social, economic, and political change in the Dominican Republic.

Poinar, George O., and Roberta Poinar. *The Amber Forest: A Reconstruction of a Vanished World.* **Princeton, NJ: Princeton University Press, 1999.**
In this book, the authors use their research on Dominican amber to reconstruct the ecosystem that existed on Hispaniola between fifteen and forty-five million years ago.

Population Reference Bureau. **September 12, 2007.**
http://www.prb.org (September 12, 2007)
The bureau offers current population figures, vital statistics, land area, and more. Special articles cover the latest environmental and health issues that concern each country.

Prado Chandler, Gary, and Liza Prado Chandler. *Dominican Republic.* **Oakland, CA: Lonely Planet Publications, 2005.**
This travel guide provides in-depth information on the Dominican Republic's wide array of natural and historical landmarks, as well as on contemporary Dominican culture. The book also includes a summary of the country's history and politics.

UNESCO Education: Dominican Republic: Education System. **2007.**
http://www.unesco.org/education/en/worldwide/latin-america (September 12, 2007)
This website links readers to basic facts on the Dominican Republic's education system, as well as statistics on school enrollment and literacy.

Veeser, Cyrus. *A World Safe for Capitalism: Dollar Diplomacy and America's Rise to Global Power.* **New York: Columbia University Press, 2002.**
This book examines U.S. business and government intervention in Dominican finances in the 1890s and the first decade of the 1900s. It shows how this period shaped not only the Dominican economy, but also U.S. foreign policy, during the following century.

The World Factbook. **September 6, 2007.**
https://www.cia.gov/library/publications/the-world-factbook/geos/dr.html (September 12, 2007)
This website features up-to-date information about the people, land, economy, and government of the Dominican Republic. It also briefly covers transnational issues.

Álvarez, Julia. *A Gift of Gracias*. **New York: Knopf, 2005.**
This picture book retells the legend of Our Lady of Altagracia, the Dominican Republic's patron saint.

Álvarez, Julia. *In the Time of the Butterflies*. **Chapel Hill, NC: Algonquin Books, 1994.**
The three Mirabal sisters, known by the code name the Butterflies, had inspired resistance to Trujillo throughout the Dominican Republic. They were brutally murdered in 1960. This novel tells their story through the lens of fiction.

Aunt Clara's Kitchen: Dominican Cooking
http://www.dominicancooking.com
This website offers a collection of typical Dominican recipes, the history and origins of Dominican cuisine, information on Dominican ingredients, cookbook reviews, reader forums, and more.

Danticat, Edwidge. *The Farming of Bones*. **New York: Penguin, 1999.**
This novel tells the story of Trujillo's 1937 Haitian genocide from the point of view of Amabelle, a Haitian servant to a Dominican family.

Díaz, Junot. *Drown*. **New York: Riverhead, 1997.**
In this acclaimed short-story collection, the author describes the modern Dominican immigrant experience. Ten stories, alternately sad, gritty, and funny, move readers from poor Dominican neighborhoods to urban communities in New York and New Jersey.

Dominican Republic
http://www.godominicanrepublic.com
This is the official site of the Dominican Republic Ministry of Tourism. In addition to practical information for travelers, it describes the country's history, arts, culture, sports, geography, climate, and more.

Dominican Republic News and Travel Information Service
http://dr1.com
This comprehensive website provides information on virtually everything Dominican—from history to current events, from blogs to podcasts, and from business directories to resort reviews.

Dominican Today
http://www.dominicantoday.com
Dominican Today is an electronic newspaper in English. It provides up-to-the-minute news on happenings in the Dominican Republic, as well as on topics of interest to Dominicans at home and abroad.

Dommermuth-Costa, Carol. *Woodrow Wilson*. **Minneapolis: Twenty-First Century Books, 2003.**
This biography follows Woodrow Wilson's career as a professor, politician, president, and founder of the League of Nations.

Embassy of the Dominican Republic in the United States
http://www.domrep.org
This website provides information tailored to Americans wishing to travel to, live in, or learn about the Dominican Republic. It includes summaries of the country's history, economy, and culture, as well as a special page for students.

Foley, Erin, and Leslie Jermyn. *Cultures of the World: Dominican Republic.* **Tarrytown, NY: Marshall Cavendish, 2005.**
This book provides an overview of Dominican geography, history, government, economy, population, lifestyle, religion, language, arts, leisure, festivals, and food. It includes political maps and full-color photographs.

Gallin, Anne, Ruth Glasser, and Jocelyn Santana. *Caribbean Connections: The Dominican Republic.* **Washington, DC: Teaching for Change, 2005.**
This book is a reader-friendly overview of the history, politics, and culture of the fourth-largest Latino community in the United States. It includes essays, oral histories, poetry, fiction, lesson plans for high school and college classrooms, and illustrated timelines and maps.

Goldstein, Margaret J. *Haiti in Pictures.* **Minneapolis: Twenty-First Century Books, 2005.**
This book examines Haiti's history, society, and culture, including its interactions with the Dominican Republic.

Gregory, Steven. *The Devil Behind the Mirror.* **Berkeley, CA: University of California Press, 2007.**
This intimate study of the residents of neighboring Dominican tourist towns provides a rare glimpse of modern Dominican culture. In particular, it reveals the effects of economic globalization on the lives and livelihoods of ordinary Dominicans.

Joseph, Lynn. *The Color of My Words.* **New York: HarperCollins, 2000.**
In this novel for young adults, Rosa, a blossoming young writer struggling with oppression in a poor seaside village in the Dominican Republic, learns that her words have the power to transform the world around her in a country where words are feared.

Ruck, Rob. *The Tropic of Baseball: Baseball in the Dominican Republic.* **Lincoln, NE: University of Nebraska Press, 1999.**
In the dirt-poor Dominican Republic, baseball is a stabilizing social force. Baseball fills the dreams of millions of Dominican boys and the hearts of everyone else. Ruck's book offers not only the flavor of Dominican baseball but a carefully crafted account of its past and present.

vgsbooks.com
http://www.vgsbooks.com
Visit vgsbooks.com, the homepage of the Visual Geography Series®. You can get linked to all sorts of useful on-line information, including geographical, historical, demographic, cultural, and economic websites. The vgsbooks.com site is a great resource for late-breaking news and statistics.

Wulffson, Don. *Before Columbus.* **Minneapolis: Twenty-First Century Books, 2007.**
This book explores the archaeological evidence for and historical theories of the exploration of the Americas by other civilizations before Columbus's 1492 landing. It discusses seven groups that may have landed on American shores between 146 B.C. to 1492.

Captions for photos appearing on cover and chapter openers:

Cover: Water plummeting over the El Limon waterfall, on the peninsula of Samana, drops 131 feet (40 m).

pp. 4–5 This beach lies on the small inlet near the mouth of Samaná Bay. Christopher Columbus named the inlet the Bay of Arrows because indigenous people forced his ships to retreat with a volley of arrows.

pp. 8–9 Small family farms fill the valleys of the Cordillera Central.

pp. 18–19 Alonso de Ojeda kidnaps a Taino. He took a number of them to Spain, where he sold them as slaves.

pp. 38–39 A Dominican artist paints a street scene in his seaside gallery.

pp. 46–47 Built in the early 1500s, the cathedral of Santa Maria la Menor is the oldest church in the New World. It is in the Colonial Zone, a UNESCO World Heritage site, in Santo Domingo.

pp. 56–57 A Santo Domingo flour mill is located on the Ozama River so it can load its products directly onto ships.

Photo Acknowledgments
The images in this book are used with the permission of: © Helene Rogers/Art Directors, pp. 4–5, 8–9, 21, 50; © XNR Publications, pp. 6, 10; © Tom Bean/CORBIS, p. 11; © Reinhard Dirscherl/Alamy, p. 14; © Paul Thompson Images/Alamy, pp. 17, 56–57; © North Wind Picture Archives, pp. 18–19; Library of Congress, pp. 23 (LC-USZ62-7862), 25 (LC-USZ61-1661); © Bettmann/CORBIS, pp. 26, 31; National Archives, pp. 28, 29, 35; © M.Torres/Travel-images.com, p. 33; AP Photo, p. 34; AP Photo/Ed Betz, p. 36; © Atlantide Phototravel/Corbis, pp. 38–39; © Tim O'Keefe/Travel Stock Photography, pp. 40, 46–47; © Philip Wolmuth/Panos Pictures, p. 41; © Orlando Barria/EFE/epa/Corbis, pp. 43, 44; © Reuters/CORBIS, p. 49; AP Photo/Tony Gutierrez, p. 53; © PCL/Alamy, p. 55; © Ellen McKnight/Alamy, p. 58; © Gideon Mendel/CORBIS, p. 61; © Richard Bickel/CORBIS, p. 62; © M. Timothy O'Keefe/Alamy, p. 63; AP Photo/The White House, Lynden R. Steele, p. 64; © Danita Delimont/Alamy, p. 65; Audrius Tomonis-www.banknotes.com, p. 68; © Laura Westlund/Independent Picture Service, p. 69.

Front cover: © Hemis/Alamy